DI200615

LASER SAILING
for Beginners and Experts

Laser Sailing

for Beginners and Experts

By Dick Tillman

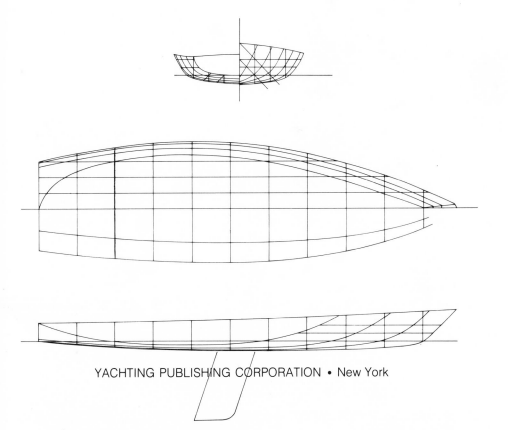

YACHTING PUBLISHING CORPORATION • New York

Contents

1   ABOUT THE LASER 11

     Some history: Two Bruces and Hans   11
     Who sails Lasers?   14
     Two basic skills: Planing and tacking   16

2   YOUR FIRST SAIL 19

     Do it in light air   19
     Capsizing and righting   20
     Reefing   20
     The five sail controls   22

3   BOAT SPEED 25

     Hull, sail, centerboard, rudder,
       and tiller maintenance   25
       hull   25
       sail   27
       instructions for application
         of sail numbers   29
       centerboard and rudder   31
       tiller   32

4   HOW TO START 33

     Practice   33
     Find the favored end   34
     Protect your lee   35
     Prepare the boat   38

5   SAILING UPWIND 39

     Keep her flat   39
     Upwind sail adjustments   42
     Waves   44

6   REACHING 45

      Board and sail adjustments   45
      Keep the helm neutral   46
      Play the waves   47
      Mark roundings   48
      Tactics   50

7   RUNNING AND JIBING 51

      Board and sail adjustment   51
      The "death roll"   53
      Jibing   55

8   PRACTICE 61

      Individual practice   61
      Boat against boat   62
      Informal racing   62
      The slalom course   65

9   GO-FAST TECHNIQUES 69

      A competitive edge   69
      Starting   69
      The compass   70
      Roll tacking   71
      Hanging in   71
      Capsizing   72
      Sail controls   74
      Humming boards and rudders   75
      Mainsheet   77
      Pumping and ooching   77
      Fixing a leak   78

10 PHYSICAL FITNESS 79

  The importance of being in shape   79
  Sail a lot   80
  The hiking bench   80

11 TRANSPORTING THE LASER 83

  Getting around   83
  Trailing   83
  Cartopping   85

12 WHAT TO WEAR 87

  Warm and cold weather   87
  Life jackets   88
  What to take to a regatta   88

13 SPORTSMANSHIP 91

  Fair and friendly competition   91
  Enjoy yourself   93

Appendix 1 The Laser
            Parts of the Boat   94
Appendix 2 Rigging Your Laser   97
Appendix 3 Further Reading   101
Appendix 4 International Laser Class Association
            Constitution and Bylaws   103
Appendix 5 Laser Construction Particulars
            The Laser Record   123
Appendix 6 The First Laser World Championship   125

To my wife Linda and my parents,
who have given so much support to me

Dick Tillman

NOBODY IS BETTER QUALIFIED THAN DICK TILLMAN to write a book about sailing and racing the Laser. He has won three Laser North American championships—the first three sailed in this exciting and rapidly growing singlehanded class—as well as Midwinter, National, North American, and French titles in the International Snipe and Finn Classes. In the 1971, 1972, and 1973 Laser North Americans, with fleets ranging in size from 89 to 135 boats, Dick won ten of 17 races, and his worst finishes were two fourths. In 1965 he was awarded the Martini and Rossi Trophy as the U.S. Yachtsman of the Year. Dick was International Snipe Class Commodore in 1972.

A 1958 graduate of the U.S. Naval Academy, whose teams won two intercollegiate national championships with his help, Dick is a Major in the U.S. Air Force, stationed at Orlando, Florida. His wife Linda enjoys sailing the Laser, and their daughters Laurie, Libbie, and Susan frequently crew for Dick in his Snipe.

CHAPTER 1

About the Laser

Some history: Two Bruces and Hans

IN ORDER TO USE THIS BOOK and enjoy the Laser to the fullest, you should know something about the Laser's background. The Laser is more than a boat, she is a concept. She is the result of the efforts of Bruce Kirby, her designer, Ian Bruce, her builder, and Hans Fogh, her sailmaker. Their objective was to create an inexpensive boat suitable for safe and fun recreational sailing and for close and challenging racing. They tried to come up with a boat that was so good in all respects that people would not want to change her. She would be sedate enough for beginners yet still give the expert an extra degree of satisfaction.

This concept began when Ian Bruce asked Bruce Kirby to design a boat that could be carried on a car's roof and that would appeal to the mass market and look better than the typical cartopper. Ian did not originally expect to be marketing the boat. Instead, he intended to produce her in his plant near Montreal for someone else. Bruce tried to sneak in a little more

The Laser was designed by Bruce Kirby, is 13'10½" overall, has a beam of 4'6", carries 76 square feet of sail, and weighs 130 pounds.

The Laser is a boat for relaxing as well as racing. Opposite, Laser builder Ian Bruce enjoys a sail with his daughter.

high performance than Ian requested, since he felt that a lively boat would always have more appeal than a relatively unresponsive one. Ian then asked Hans to design the sail. Everyone involved had a tremendous amount of expertise to contribute to the boat. Hans had won the Flying Dutchman World Championship and a silver medal in the Olympics, and Ian and Bruce were champion International 14 sailors and had both represented Canada in the Olympics.

Ever since the Laser was first marketed in North America in January, 1971, the boat has received an exceptionally warm reception in every country in which she has been introduced. I feel that the success of the boat is due to a blend of several factors: her clever but simple design; her clean appearance and quality workmanship; her strong class development; and her unique world-wide manufacturing and distribution system. Given the boat and the concept, it is no wonder that the class has enjoyed an unprecedented growth rate.

Hans Loffel

Who sails Lasers?

I have found that those who enjoy and sail Lasers fall into three fairly distinct groups. The majority sails the boat for recreation. Others buy her for fun racing near their homes. And some "super racers" race Lasers seriously at major regional, national, and international regattas. This book is for all three groups.

Many Laser owners are recreational sailors who do not race. Sailing is one of the finest forms of recreation available. It offers relaxation, fresh air, and exercise. It also instills confidence and satisfaction in the young and the old alike. Have you ever seen the expression of someone who has just mastered a tack or jibe for the first time? Do you remember your own feeling of accomplishment when you first felt really comfortable in a boat?

The Laser is fine for the recreational sailor because she is safe, lightweight, and responsive. If you are a new sailor, you need not worry about capsizing—not that it cannot happen, but because if it does the boat will neither swamp nor sink. You can right her by yourself and continue to sail. The Laser is light, with a designed hull weight of 130 pounds. Two people can easily handle her onshore and launch and retrieve her. The third characteristic which sets the Laser apart from most other boats is her responsiveness. Trimming the sail produces rapid acceleration and a change of helm causes an instant response.

This book should help the beginner or strictly recreational sailor to master the sailing techniques and also to care for and get the most enjoyment out of the Laser. Somewhere along the way, however, most sailors become intrigued with the idea of racing.

Many racers who own Lasers have learned to sail in other classes and buy the Laser with the intention of racing. Some have done their first sailing and racing in a Laser. If you add the most enthusiastic recreational sailors, the racing set is then the largest in number of the three groups who sail the Laser. And so it should be, since this is what the boat was designed for.

Hans Loffel

Sailors from all over the world gathered for the first Laser World Championship in 1974 in Bermuda for great racing . . . and a good time.

Burmuda News Bureau,
Eric Johnson

The manufacturer states, "Once beginners have learned the basics, they have a bonus in store. They will be pleasantly surprised to find that this boat is no stepping stone but has been carefully designed and rigged to satisfy and challenge the most demanding enthusiast."

One of my biggest thrills as an experienced racer of some 25 years was my first sail in a Laser. This occurred in 1971 when the U.S. Olympic Committee had assembled the members of the Pan American Games sailing team in Miami to board charter planes to Colombia. There was a spare day available, and I was invited to sail a Snipe in the local fleet races. The Laser dealer sailed by in his boat after the races and asked me to try her. After the first minute in the boat I said, "This is for me!" I had never had such satisfaction in a boat and that experience has led to many hours of good local and international racing. This book is written to pass on to other racing sailors and "super racers" some techniques and advice to help sail a Laser fast.

The "super racers" belong to the third group of Laser sailors. While racers all have one thing in common in liking to race, the super racers want to excel. These are the particularly enthusiastic helmsmen who are motivated toward becoming expert sailors in this and other classes. But why in a Laser?

Two basic skills: Planing and tacking

First of all, the Laser has many similarities to larger, more expensive high performance boats. For instance, in the Laser you learn very quickly that to go fast on a planing reach you must (1) have the vang on tight, (2) keep the boat absolutely flat, and (3) raise the centerboard at least halfway. The difference between those who are sailing properly and those who are not is painfully obvious. In all good boats, when you trim, balance, and sail the boat correctly, the reward is speed and performance. When you do not, you clearly have the "slows."

Another example: when beating in winds above 12-15

Vang tight, boat flat, and centerboard half-way up, 1973 U.S. Youth Champion and 1974 World Champion Peter Commette planes fast. A length of shock cord led to the mast helps keep the board up.

John Rousmaniere

knots, you learn from experience that the sail must be as flat and trimmed as far to leeward as you can get it. To do this you must (1) tighten the outhaul to create a definite curl at the foot of the sail when the boat is head to wind, (2) pull the traveler and Cunningham as tight as they will go, (3) sheet in hard, and (4) hike as hard as is necessary to hold the boat flat. These techniques applied to most other centerboarders will produce definite improvements in speed.

One of the most valuable motor skills is tacking properly. In winds over ten knots, you must tack fast and smoothly to do well. Develop a good technique and stick to it. One procedure in a boat equipped with a centermounted ratchet block and two cleats on the side deck is (1) before starting the tack and while still hiking, ease the mainsheet ten to 12 inches, (2) push the tiller to leeward, (3) quickly shift to the opposite side of the boat while moving the tiller smoothly to leeward and changing hands on the sheet and tiller, (4) immediately hike enough to flatten the boat while pushing the tiller down to the centerline and trimming the mainsheet, (5) check for nearby boats. You should face forward while you move across the boat. With some practice, you will learn how to switch hands on the tiller behind your back. The ratchet block will take much of the load off the sheet and make it easy to change sheet hands simultaneously.

If your boat has the optional center-mounted cam cleat, you may tack facing either forward or aft, but in either case it is a good idea to keep the sheet uncleated to avoid capsizes if the wind is at all strong.

In a Laser, one can get considerably more practice per hour than in other, more sophisticated classes. You can launch, rig, and be ready to sail in a much shorter time than in other types of boats. Also, the boat is ideal for frostbite sailing during the winter if the skipper is properly dressed.

I have tried to analyze the reasons why people sail Lasers. The simple explanation is that it is fun, whether for recreational sailors, racers or super racers. So let's get on with the sailing part of the book.

CHAPTER 2

Your First Sail

Do it in light air

ONE OF THE MOST EXCITING EXPERIENCES a sailor can have is his first sail in a new boat. This is particularly true with a Laser. The inexperienced helmsman may be in for some excitement if his first sail is on a windy day, but even the most experienced sailor will be challenged by the boat until he acquires the proper feel.

No matter whether you are a recreational sailor, a racer, or a super racer, I recommend taking the Laser out for the first time in light to moderate wind (six to ten knots) and smooth seas. The boat will be responsive under these conditions, and you can easily and safely become familiar with the operation of the centerboard and use of the Cunningham, outhaul, clew tie-down, vang, and traveler controls. If it is too windy, you will be busy keeping the boat under control, and you may capsize before you have everything figured out.

Capsizing and righting

Everyone capsizes sooner or later. If you do, righting the boat is simple. You need only put your weight on the centerboard and the boat will right herself. A note of caution: if it is windy, you should swing the bow of the boat into or slightly beyond the wind before righting. If you do not, she will keep on coming as she rights and tip over on top of you. When this happens, you must swim either under or around the boat and repeat the procedure. After you right the boat, climb into the cockpit and sail away. The cockpit will be dry because any water in it will have run out while the boat was on her side. It is a good idea to secure loose gear such as your sponge, water scoop, and paddle so that they do not float away if you capsize.

If you happen to turn turtle (a 180° capsize where the hull is completely upside down), you must climb up on the windward side to pull on the centerboard. The boat may take a bit longer to come up, but don't worry, she will.

Reefing

The biggest thrill of owning a planing dinghy is to sail her in strong winds. Tony Herrmann, the well-known U.S. Finn sailor, came up with a practical method of handling the Laser in strong winds. This should be particularly appealing to anyone weighing less than 150 pounds who finds the boat overpowering in winds over 20 knots. Tony's technique is to put reefs into the sail at the mast. Do this by disconnecting the Cunningham, outhaul, and vang, and rotating the mast and sail two or three turns. One turn only tightens the leech and does not help. If you use two turns, the top batten may be left in place and the sail sets well. For three turns you must remove the top batten and expect some distortion in the sail. Reconnect the Cunningham, boom (you may need a longer outhaul), and vang, and you have a boat that is not only controllable in strong winds with no excessive helm but is responsive and seaworthy as well.

Carl Van Duyne

Under reefed main, a sailor accelerates through some big seas in a typical San Francisco Bay blow. Below, two teenagers race a reefed Laser together at the 1973 Midwinters off Miami. Two may race in one boat if they sail together throughout the entire series and do not alternate as skipper.

John Weber

Dick Tillman is pictured about to tack in a five-knot wind. The sail controls are properly adjusted.

John Rousmaniere

At the opposite extreme, if there is not enough wind to maintain steerageway it is impossible to really enjoy the boat. The Laser responds as well as any boat in light air, but no boat is fun to sail if there is not enough wind to fill the sail. Nevertheless, taking the boat out in smooth water for the first sail can help you become familiar with the controls. Sailing in a chop or sea will demand that you pay more attention to balancing and controlling the boat than to observing the effect of the adjustments on the sail.

The five sail controls

I am stressing the sail controls because understanding their use will increase both the enjoyment and success of your sailing. Some controls are helpful for sailing the boat safely; others are essential for getting maximum performance. Since all are im-

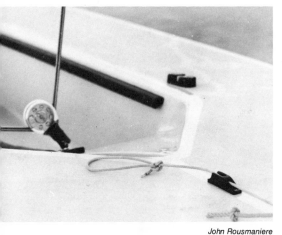

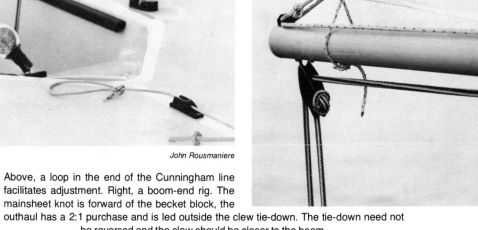

Above, a loop in the end of the Cunningham line facilitates adjustment. Right, a boom-end rig. The mainsheet knot is forward of the becket block, the outhaul has a 2:1 purchase and is led outside the clew tie-down. The tie-down need not be reversed and the clew should be closer to the boom.

portant to the racing sailor, a brief description is in order.

Boom Vang. The vang, or kicker, is a most important adjustment. It holds the boom down and maintains a firm leech when reaching and running. It is a good idea to disconnect the vang when you tie up to the dock or leave the boat unattended so the sail will not fill and cause the boat to capsize. Under sail it should always be attached in order to keep the boom on the gooseneck. The vang should be tightened as the wind increases, although there are exceptions to this rule.

Cunningham. This line controls the fore and aft position of the point of maximum draft in the sail. Generally the Cunningham should be tightened when beating in order to move the draft forward and should be eased when off the wind to let the draft move aft. Upwind, the Cunningham should be tightened as the wind increases. It is a good idea to put a loop in the end of the Cunningham line. This prevents it from slipping through the clam cleat and makes it easier to adjust. It is possible to lose the mast after a capsize if the Cunningham is not cleated.

Outhaul. The outhaul controls the amount of draft, or fullness, in a sail. Most Laser sailors leave too much slack in the outhaul, which makes the sail too full. Generally, you should tighten the outhaul enough to put a slight curl in the foot of the sail. Like the vang and the Cunningham, the outhaul should be tightened as the wind increases.

Clew tie-down. The function of this small diameter line, which is supplied with two small brummel hooks attached, is to hold the clew of the sail close to the boom. The tie-down is not necessary for recreational sailing, but it improves speed in racing because it increases the mainsheet's control of leech tension.

Traveler. The traveler controls the lateral plane of the sail relative to the centerline of the boat. This is an extremely important control when it comes to racing, though many sailors tend to ignore it. On a beat, when the traveler is loose, the sail positions itself toward the centerline of the boat. When it is tight, the sail can be trimmed further to leeward. Herein lies the secret of success of many heavy air experts. When the wind is blowing over 12 knots or when you cannot hike the boat flat, tighten the traveler and push the boom to leeward.

A more complete description of these controls and their uses is outlined in later chapters and summarized in the Table on page 42.

CHAPTER 3

Boat Speed

Hull, sail, centerboard, rudder, and tiller maintenance

ALTHOUGH THE LASER IS THE EPITOME of the strict one-design principle, there are still a few things you can do to make one Laser go faster than another. Psychologically, you can sail your best race only when you know that everything about your boat is right. Therefore you must exert maximum effort on things you control; when it comes to things you cannot control such as wind and waves, you can only hope to sail as well as or a little better than your competition. For example, if your centerboard is rough, you can and should wetsand it. But if the wind lifts the fleet 30 degrees when you are to leeward on the last beat, you can't do much about that. So let's discuss those things that you can control: hull, sail, centerboard, rudder, and tiller.

Hull. The Laser is solidly constructed but, at about 130 pounds, she is still a relatively light boat. Although she has more than adequate strength while in the water and can be sailed hard, she does require some care when ashore.

The hull should be properly supported when stored on

Two Lasers piggy-backed on a trailer, each supported at the mast hole and at the after end of the cockpit.

either a dolly or a trailer. The strongest points of the hull are the keel section under the mast step and the rounded turn of the bilge at the after end of the cockpit. The boat should be supported at these points to avoid deflection and permanent deformation of the hull. Better still, the boat can be supported under the gunwale. A new launching trolley which supports the boat only under the gunwale at mid point and at the bow has been designed for this purpose.

A safe way to store the boat is upside down, with the forward support at or under the mast hole and the aft support at the after end of the cockpit. The supports should either conform to the deck curve—1"x4" pine board will do—or be well padded. An alternate method is to lean the boat on her sheer against a wall.

Assuming the boat is stored properly, the only other maintenance requirement is to keep the hull clean and smooth. Exactly how smooth is open to question. A poor finish will not prevent you from winning. At the 1965 North American Finn Championship held in Bermuda, Pete Barrett and I both sailed Finns supplied by the United States International Sailing Association (USISA). In the first race both boats had bad scratches and dirt all over their bottoms. We finished in the top two positions, although the wind was light. We then wetsanded the boats to make them faster, but it really did not seem to make a lot of difference. I believe the Laser is similar to the Finn in that there are many other, more important, factors in winning than a super-smooth bottom. I have noticed one thing, however. Those who take the most pride in their equipment and take care of it are generally out in front.

Sail. Since the sail is the driving force of the boat, it deserves attention. You do not need to worry about a competitor having a better designed sail than you. When Hans Fogh completed the design of the sail, he committed that design to Mylar patterns from which all sails were cut, ensuring to the maximum extent possible that every sail has the same shape. Class rules prohibit recutting of sails. Now the boat's builder, Performance Sailcraft, is cutting sails by a computer operated

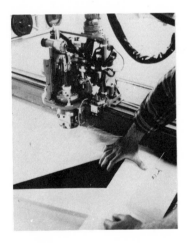

Graham Hall

Laser sails are now cut to exacting standards by a Gerber numerical cutter at Chesapeake Cutters Inc. in Annapolis, Maryland. Right, the cutting head of the machine with rotating turret operates above a bristle vacuum table.

 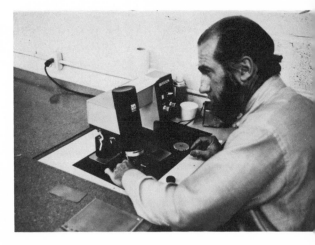

Graham Hall

Above, sails are laid out for shipment. Right, Jack Lynch, president of Chesapeake
Cutters Inc., operates the sonic Dacron "welder" which secures the taped seams to
prevent alteration of the one-design shape.

machine, the coordinates for which have been taken from the
Mylar patterns. This brings the tolerances down to three one-
thousandths of an inch. The second part of the program in-
volves seaming the sails ultrasonically so that the shape is fixed.
The sail is then shipped in this condition to various sailmakers
serving different plant locations throughout the world, who,
under contractual obligation, must complete the sail in strict
accordance with instructions prepared by Hans Fogh.

When new, the sails are as similar as anyone can make
them. However, no sail will maintain its finish and texture or
hold its shape forever, no matter how carefully you treat it. If
you are a serious racer, you might consider having two sails,
one for practice and one for major regattas. A good way to
extend the life of the sail is to fold it carefully after each use in
the same way it was folded when new. Don't let it luff unneces-
sarily. Never cram it into the bag or the car trunk, and avoid
exposing it to the sun for prolonged periods.

When you race, the numbers on the sail must correspond
to the first five digits stamped on the boat's transom or to the

numbers stamped under the bow eye. Sail numbers are available from your dealer or a sailmaker. You can also make them yourself using self-adhesive fabric or stencil them on with a waterproof felt-tipped pen. If you use the numbers supplied by your dealer, the following instructions should help in applying them.

Instructions for application of sail numbers. Before you start, find a clean working surface. A large table or a clean, smooth floor is ideal. If your sail has been used, the fourth panel from the head of the sail should be sponged clean with a mild soap and warm water to be sure there is no grime or dust on the surface. Both sides should be clean.

The rules of the International Yacht Racing Union specify that the numbers shall be placed at different heights on the two sides of the sail, those on the starboard side being uppermost. To find the starboard side of the sail, put it on the floor with the luff sleeve on your right. This way, the starboard side is up.

Draw a pencil line parallel to and 15¾" (40 cm) below the top seam of the fourth panel. The line should start about 4" (10 cm) from the leech of the sail and be about 48" (120 cm) long. This line will locate the bottom edge of the numbers on the starboard side.

Before peeling off the paper backing, place and space the numbers in their proper order, starting 4" (10 cm) from the leech. There should be 2" (5 cm) between each number. When you are happy with the way they look, carefully trace them on the sail with a pencil.

Now peel off about 1½" (4 cm) of protective paper from the bottom edge of the number, bend it back and carefully locate the number on the sail (don't press yet) in the appropriate tracing. You don't have more than two chances to properly locate it squarely. Now smooth out the peeled portion by pressing firmly with your thumb. You can now continue peeling the protective paper along the full width of the number. It should fall naturally into the traced area. Rub the number down hard, paying particular attention to the edges. Make sure there are no wrinkles or bubbles. Apply the other numbers to the starboard side.

Turn the sail over and flatten it. Draw another line 15¾″ (40 cm) below the bottom line of the starboard numbers. This

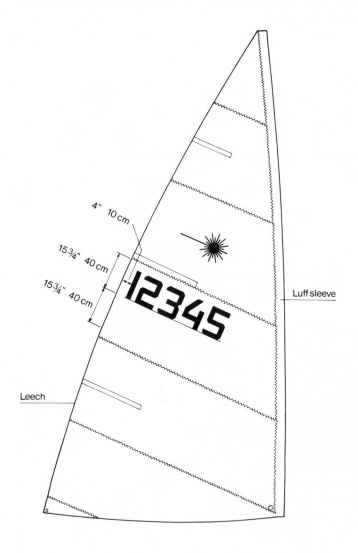

line is the bottom edge of the port side numbers. This time, the numbers read from the luff sleeve towards the leech; you should therefore start with the last number in the sequence, 4″ (10 cm) from the leech and work backwards. Trace the numbers out and apply them in the same way.

Give the adhesive a chance to dry; don't use your sail for 24 hours. Properly applied, your numbers will stay put for a long time.

Centerboard and rudder. These are the only items that require periodic maintenance. Since they comprise a substantial portion of the underwater surface of the boat, they also deserve special treatment and attention. Smooth leading and trailing edges are essential for minimizing drag. To fill dents and gouges, use wood dough if the board is wood, or resin if it is fiberglass. Refinish the board and rudder as often as needed, being sure to wetsand after refinishing. I use #400 wet or dry sandpaper, followed by #600, keeping the surface and the paper wet as I sand. The centerboard is quite important and you should get the best possible finish on yours and carry it with you if you want to sail in regattas in a borrowed boat. Most Laser dealers have carry-all bags designed to protect rudders and centerboards. Use them for extra protection.

When racing, the quicker you can get the board up after you round the weather mark the better off you will be. If it is hard to slide up and down, the rubber snubbing block at the after end of the trunk probably binds too much against the board. Here is how you can adjust it. With the boat in the water, back out the two screws holding the rubber. Place the board in the trunk and while they and the rubber are wet, slowly reseat the rubber, testing for the correct tension as you turn the screws down. The new boats come with a flat V-shaped rubber snubber which is easily adjusted by moving fore and aft. An alternative is to remove the rubber entirely. If you remove it, you should use a length of shock cord to hold the board in position and keep it in place in case of a capsize. Attach the shock cord to the upper forward corner of the board and to the

boom vang bale on the mast or the Cunningham eye on the deck
at the mast. A spot of white bathroom tile sealer at the forward
edge of the trunk works well in conjunction with the shock cord
as a stop.

Tiller. The tiller should fit into the rudder tightly. You can
get a much better "feel" when there is no slop between the tiller
and rudder. If necessary you can insert a thin wood wedge or
wrap tape around the tiller to insure a tight fit.

Although the tiller extension supplied by the builder is
satisfactory, there are times going downwind in very light air
when you need to get your weight forward of the centerboard
and the stock extension will not be long enough to reach. A
good substitute is an extendable hiking stick. This allows you to
sit forward of the board in winds under three knots and still
steer the boat comfortably. Peter Commette, who won the first
Laser World Championship in Bermuda in 1974, uses a long
tiller extension made from PVC plastic tubing. It is the same
length as the tiller and has a universal fitting on one end and a
rubber cap on the other. It can be passed under the boom
when tacking by swiveling it forward during the tack.

In this chapter we have discussed how to care for, maintain, and adjust the boat and her sail in the interest of ensuring
the greatest possible speed. Although each suggestion may be
minor in itself, following them all may help you sail significantly faster than your less dedicated competitor. The
psychological advantage alone will better prepare you for competition. Ideas on starting and sailing a Laser fast on the beat,
the reach, and the run follow in the next four chapters.

CHAPTER 4

How to Start

Practice

THE CLOSENESS OF THE COMPETITION during the starting maneuvers—the sheer excitement of it—and the importance that one's start has in the final outcome, make this the most critical, interesting, and often the most nerve-shattering part of racing. How good your position is at and immediately after the start is dependent upon practice, planning and preparation.

The best starters are those who have practiced the most. Practicing is easy. All you need is another boat besides your own. A good way to practice is to set up a starting line, give a two-minute preparatory signal, and start. After one boat has clearly gained an advantage over the other either by establishing a safe leeward or by driving over the leeward boat, go back and start again. This way you can get a dozen practice starts in a short time. You learn to control the boat better and profit from each mistake you make. You can simulate starting in a larger fleet by shortening the length of the line. Three or more boats will of course provide a more realistic situation.

Peter Commette concentrates at the start of one of the races at the first Laser World Championship in Bermuda.

Bermuda News Bureau, Eric Johnson

Find the favored end

For an official race, decide where on the line you want to start. This means getting out to the starting area 20 to 30 minutes beforehand and becoming familiar with the wind and sea conditions. Make some runs at the line to see how long it takes to get there from a given point. You can also determine if the wind is oscillating or persistently shifting. Doing well at the start is a matter of being in phase with the shifts. A compass helps here. The easiest way to determine the favored end of the line in relation to the shifts is to head up until the boat is perpendicular to the line. On that heading the boom will be pointing toward the favored end. If the boom remains on the centerline, you know that the line is square to the wind and neither end has an advantage. Then you consider any oscillating shifts you have observed. For example, if the wind is shifting every 15 minutes and ten minutes ago the buoy end was favored but now, five minutes before the start, the line is square, you may assume that at the start the committee boat end will be favored.

Another way to find the favored end is to sail down the line with the sail eased as far as possible and still full. When you reach the end of the line, tack and head back toward the other end without changing the trim. If the sail is luffing, you are headed toward the favored end. If you can ease the sail, you are headed away from the favored end.

There are a few other points to consider. If you are known to have local knowledge or if you are the series leader, you can expect a few of your competitors to follow you. Therefore you should not make it obvious to the rest of the competition exactly where you intend to start. On the other hand, if you are not certain where to start, you might try to stay close to a local expert. Another factor to consider is the crowd of boats that usually clog up one end of the line. Generally, it is better to avoid tangling with this group. Also, one side of the course may be heavily favored because of a persistent shift or a peculiar current. One or more of these factors may dictate a start somewhere other than at the "favored end"—for instance, in the middle.

Another point to consider in starting is the number of boats on the line. At both the first Laser North American Championship at Baltimore in 1971 and the first Midwinter Championship at Charleston in 1972, there were over 85 starters. In a fleet this size, if you do not get away from the starting line in clear air you are hurting. This is when it is important to have a good start.

Protect your lee

The most important concern in starting is to protect your lee. About ten to 20 seconds before the gun, discourage anyone from coming up on your leeward side. At the same time, try to pinch the boats off your windward quarter up to windward. You want to establish a space of about a boat length to leeward into which you can drive off a few seconds before the start.

Should the line be long and the fleet large and should you

The author raced a Laser at "Yachting's" 1974 One-of-a-Kind Regatta and got an excellent start. Number 1666 is too far to leeward to bother him and soon Dick will backwind number 300.

decide to start in the middle, you may not have to worry about protecting your lee. Instead, line up with the boats to windward and to leeward and then sheet in to get underway about ten to 15 seconds before the start. There will nearly always be a sag in the middle of the line since the other sailors will be afraid of starting early. By getting a boat length lead over the others you will have a clear air start.

Don't be afraid of getting a front row seat. In a large fleet there is rarely enough room to accommodate everyone at the favored end of the line. You must be prepared to get to the front and stay very close to the line as early as the preparatory signal, and from this position you must protect your lee. Those caught behind with only a minute or two before the start may find it impossible to locate a hole and end up having to take a lot of bad air.

Starting in the 109-boat fleet at the first Laser Worlds called for specialized techniques. Note dip in the middle of the line.

On the other hand, if the fleet is small and you have not had much experience in starting, you should have good success with the classic starting method. Between one and two minutes before the start, sail downwind on port tack through the starting line at the place you have planned to start. Check the time remaining. Tack five seconds (this is the approximate time it takes to tack a Laser) before half of the time remaining has elapsed. Then sail for the line on a starboard tack and you should have a well-timed, good start, provided other boats do not interfere with you.

If you find yourself too high on the line before the start or if a current is pushing you across, a good technique is to raise the centerboard and drift to leeward.

Don't forget to take a look to windward six or seven minutes before the start to spot any major shifts or changes in wind velocity. You can usually identify either of these conditions by a change in the shade of the water or by observing smoke, flags, or other boats sailing in a new wind.

Prepare the boat

After you have planned where and how to start, the next step is to prepare the boat for the start. Check the centerboard and rudder for weeds. Make final adjustments to the outhaul, traveler, vang, and Cunningham. It is important to have the boat ready in all respects to go at maximum speed beginning five to ten seconds before the starting gun in medium and heavy air and 15 to 20 seconds before the gun in light air or drifting conditions. If you have to move in from a hiking position after starting to tighten the Cunningham, you will probably lose a half a boat length on the boat to windward, which could then drive over you. Don't give an inch at the start. It is disastrous to let someone climb over you or throw backwind toward you from leeward. This slows you just enough to let the next boat pass and the next and the next.

If you get a mediocre start, tack into clear air as soon as possible. You do not want other boats interfering with your wind. Your objective when starting is to be sailing at top speed in clear air two minutes after the gun.

CHAPTER 5

Sailing Upwind

Keep her flat

RACES ARE WON on the windward leg. It is essential to be in the running at the first windward mark in order to place well in the race. Therefore it is of primary importance to develop speed and technique when sailing hard on the wind. Let's consider the factors of speed and technique when sailing to weather in medium, drifting, and heavy weather conditions.

Medium Air (five to 15 knots). The cardinal rule is to keep the boat perfectly flat at all times. In the five- to ten-knot range you will want to have the traveler adjusted about halfway out. In the ten- to 15-knot range the traveler should be tight to allow the boom to go to the maximum leeward position. The mainsheet in each case should be as tight as possible to induce maximum bend in the mast. A figure-eight knot at the end of the sheet going to the boom block becket will enable the boom block and the traveler blocks to meet. Though the vang should be adjusted medium to tight, it is not really in use when beating. You need to preadjust it the proper amount only for offwind legs.

The Cunningham needs constant attention as the wind changes. Luff wrinkles should barely be pulled out. As the wind lightens, ease the Cunningham until there are tiny wrinkles in the luff. This adjustment allows the draft to move aft. When the wind freshens, pull it in to remove luff wrinkles and move the deepest part of the sail forward. The position of the outhaul is also important but normally you set it before the race and then leave it alone. Be sure to put a knot toward the end of the line which exits the clam cleat on the boom. It is possible for the end to catch in the cleat, and then it is very difficult to move it either way.

Drifting Conditions (zero to three knots). Racing in light air requires precise trimming and much practice. The key is proper sheet tension. The traveler should be tight, the vang and the Cunningham loose. The outhaul should be adjusted so as to be just short of putting a curl in the foot of the sail. With the traveler tight, push the boom to leeward and put just enough tension on the sheet to bend the mast slightly and move the draft of the sail aft. Too much tension will tighten the leech excessively, not enough will allow the sail to hang shapelessly from the mast. Unlike sailing upwind in medium and heavy winds, you should heel the boat 5-10 degrees to leeward in drifting conditions. Center your weight forward, just over or alongside the centerboard or, even better, up against the mast. (Remember that the class rules do not allow you to be forward of the mast.)

The sailor who concentrates on keeping his boat moving by sailing slightly off the wind with the boom to leeward with slight tension on the sheet will move rapidly past someone who is trying to point too close to the wind with his sail sheeted in tight.

Of course it helps to know where the wind is coming from in drifting conditions. It is useful to have a telltale or wind indicator. A masthead fly is helpful. Some skippers use the Tillman Teller, designed by the author. It is simply a sensitive wind indicator mounted on the deck at the bow that tells the

Bermuda News Bureau, Eric Johnson
Some good form is illustrated here as these sailors move out to windward in puffy wind.

sailor the correct heading through a pair of indicators. The indicators react to the slightest windshift and, by aligning the indicators, the sailor is assured of steering at the optimum angle to the wind.

Keeping the boat on the wind and keeping her moving are the secrets to sailing to windward in a drifter.

Strong Air (15 to 30 knots). In heavy weather, the person who comes closest to holding his boat completely flat will move the fastest. To make this easier, the traveler, outhaul, and Cunningham should be as tight as you can make them. To do this, grab the traveler with both hands, throw your weight against it, and pull it as far as it will come. This will shorten the traveler and let the boom slide toward the lee rail. The effect is to reduce the heeling moment and increase forward speed. Tighten the outhaul so that the foot of the sail is drum tight. This reduces the draft of the sail, which in turn decreases the heeling force. Put both hands on the Cunningham and pull back. It must be tight to move the draft of the sail forward; check to be sure the line does not slip in the clam cleat.

The vang, sheet, and centerboard require adjustment to a degree. Adjust the vang by kneeling on the deck and pushing the boom down with one hand while pulling the vang tight with

Upwind Sail Adjustments

Sail Controls	Drifter (0-3 mph)	Light Wind (3-5 mph)	Medium Wind (5-10 mph)	(10-15 mph)	Heavy Wind (15 mph & up)
Sheet	medium	medium	tight	two-block	medium
Traveler	tight	medium	medium	tight	very tight
Vang	loose	loose	medium	tight	tight
Cunningham	loose	loose	medium	tight	very tight
Outhaul	no curl	no curl	slight curl	medium tight	very tight
from foot to boom	4 inches	4 inches	2 inches	1 inch	0 inches

the other hand. If you are light, overvanging is harmful as it creates a tight leech which increases weather helm and heeling moment. Sheet in and hike hard to bend the mast tip to leeward, which in turn reduces the heeling moment. Here, too, if you are light, oversheeting and causing a tight leech is harmful. The centerboard may be raised three to four inches, allowing

John Rousmaniere

Tillman keeps her flat as he responds to puffs in Newport Harbor, California, after a race at the 1974 One-of-a-Kind Regatta. Note adjustments for medium wind in the table on page 42.

the boat to pass through the waves easier and reducing some of
the lateral resistance which contributes to the heeling moment.

If you weigh less than 160 pounds, you may need to play
the sheet to keep from heeling excessively in puffs. The key is
to keep the boat flat, not to keep the sail full. Trim the sheet for
the puffs and lulls. A ratchet block, which is an approved piece
of optional gear, will help because it eases the load on the sheet
in your hand. You should also consider wearing the maximum
weight allowed by the class rules (see rule 27 in the appendix).
Remember that all other things being equal, whoever hikes the
hardest will go the fastest. This also means being in top physical
shape to get maximum performance from the Laser.

Waves

Heavy winds and heavy seas normally go hand in hand. In
these conditions, as in the drifting beats, it does not pay to
pinch. To do so merely creates leeway at the expense of forward motion. It is better to power through the waves—even
though heeling somewhat—than to pinch or luff. The best
technique is to steer an "S" course through the waves by alternately heading up into the crests and bearing off as the crests
pass under the boat. Bearing off means bringing the tiller
forceably and rapidly to windward while at the same time hiking a bit harder. The result is not so much actual bearing off as
steering the boat to her former course by kicking the stern to
windward.

A table summarizing the adjustments of the sail controls
for various wind conditions appears on page 42. However, the
most significant factor that affects boat speed is not shown: this
is the ability of the skipper to keep the boat flat in all but
drifting conditions. This factor is also the key to success in
sailing the boat fast on reaches and runs, subjects which are
covered in the next two chapters.

CHAPTER 6

Reaching

Board and sail adjustments

REACHING IS CERTAINLY THE MOST EXHILARATING POINT of sail in a Laser. It also presents a prime opportunity for increasing a lead or catching up, as the case may be. The difference in speed between the good and not so good Laser sailor is greatest on this leg of the course. It is easier for a lighter person to hold the boat flat on a reach than when going upwind since the boat's heeling moment is considerably less. In this chapter we will look at techniques for maximizing speed, rounding marks and passing boats.

First, some basic pointers for achieving speed on a reach which apply for all ranges of wind. In reaching you always have the centerboard up, with about 18″ showing above deck—a few inches less for a close reach and a few inches more for a broad reach. You should position the board at the point where the boat is just short of making leeway (sliding to leeward). The vang should be tight and the Cunningham loose. Some sailors ease the outhaul if they are confident that they can get it back in again for sailing upwind.

Keep the helm neutral

The wind strength determines where you put your weight. The lighter the wind, the further forward you want to be. Thus, in a drifter (0-3 knots), you should be up against the mast (but no part of your body is allowed ahead of it). In light air (3-5 knots), you would be at the forward end of the cockpit. In medium air (5-15 knots), position yourself in the middle of the cockpit and in heavy air move toward the stern. In any case, it is extremely important in all wind conditions to balance the boat so that the helm is neutral. That is, the boat should track straight if you release the tiller. If she has weather helm and starts to swing into the wind (as she probably will) you need to hold the boat flatter or possibly heel her slightly to windward. This position may feel awkward, but it is the right one for most singlehanded dinghies. The boat must be sailed flat to eliminate resistance caused by pressure on the rudder. On reaches, in light to medium air, the best sailors steer delicately, with thumb and index finger on the tiller or a light touch on the tiller extension.

In light air, it is important to keep your weight forward to lift the stern and reduce wetted surface.

John Rousmaniere

Bermuda News Bureau, Roland Skinner

The reach presents a prime opportunity for gaining ground, once one masters the technique.

Play the waves

In rough sea conditions, you can make tremendous gains by playing the waves. Since the average skipper weighs nearly half again as much as the boat, he can control the boat to a large degree with his own movement·in the cockpit. The trick is to work or steer the boat down or across the waves much as a surfer coasts down the slope of a wave. This often requires vigorous tiller action and fore and aft and sideways movement in the boat as well as fast trimming with the sheet. Concentrate on steering into the trough of the wave by bearing off with it as the crest comes under the stern. At the same time keep the sail properly trimmed and balance the boat, often heeling her to windward. As you lose a wave, head up, trimming as you do, and catch the next wave as it passes underneath. Then lean forward and bear away sharply on the top, easing the sheet in the process and again heeling to windward. The feeling is sensational when you catch a good one and you will know when you have done it right. All this takes practice but it pays big dividends in the offwind legs. Concentration and balance are the critical factors.

Mark roundings

Now for rounding the marks—windward mark first, reaching and leeward marks second. When the mark is to be left to port, the rounding will be smoother and faster if you approach on the starboard tack layline rather than on the port tack layline. Ease the sheet smartly and keep the boat flat as you swing onto the new course. If she heels, you will have problems steering. As soon as you are around the mark, raise the centerboard and ease the Cunningham. The advantage of rounding in this manner is that you do not lose momentum. A 180-degree rounding maneuver after approaching on the port tack leaves you practically dead in the water by the time you have tacked and borne off.

Now you are heading for the reaching mark and then for the leeward mark to complete the triangle. At both, it is important to approach the mark wide so as to pass it close aboard as you head for the next one. By doing so, you prevent or at least discourage another sailor who has no legal buoy room from sneaking in between you and the mark. You also keep moving at maximum possible speed with no sharp maneuvers.

When rounding the leeward mark, it is necessary to pull in a lot of sheet as you harden up for the beat. The faster you can get the sheet in, the better you will do. At the same time, however, you must have complete control of the helm so that you can steer smoothly around the mark. Here is a good technique for doing this. As you approach the mark on port tack, push the board down, waiting until the last possible moment to do it. Then quickly yank on the Cunningham. Your right hand will be holding the tiller extension. The sheet will be in your left hand. As you round the mark, sheet in with your left hand by pulling the line across your chest and placing it in your right hand (which you are also using to steer the boat). Hold the sheet in your right hand and repeat the process, dropping the excess line into the cockpit, until you are fully sheeted in. With practice, you can develop this into a smooth maneuver.

Hans Loffel

A smooth mark rounding can mean the difference between gaining or losing a great deal of ground.

Tactics

Now what should you do if you are about to pass a boat on one of the reaching legs? I can offer a few rules of thumb.

(1) If you are going to pass to windward, do so with at least 30 feet (about two boat lengths) between you and the boat you are passing. This discourages or prevents the other boat from luffing you.

(2) If you are going to pass to leeward, do so at least two boat lengths away. This keeps you out of the other's blanket zone.

(3) Head straight for the next mark, except in two cases. One, if there are a lot of boats going around the weather mark, try to stay above them (on their wind). Two, if practicable, try to approach a downwind mark well to leeward of a group of boats. Then as you come up for the mark, you will be sailing closer to the wind with greater speed and, on the first reach, you will be on the inside of the mark where you can take advantage of buoy room rights. You can normally pick up a number of boats on a reach by sailing this S-shaped course between the buoys.

(4) If there is a current, be aware of which direction it is pushing you and adjust your course so that you are always on a line between the two buoys. The number of good sailors who neglect this point is surprising, even though it is difficult at times to predetermine the drift of the current. As soon as you get around the buoy, check your position on the rhumb line in relation to other boats on the leg. It is usually obvious which way the current is flowing and you can adjust your course accordingly.

Getting the most speed out of the boat on reaches, rounding marks smoothly without losing momentum, and knowing how to pass other boats will go a long way toward earning you a top position in a race. Now let's move to the final, and perhaps the most thrilling, leg of the course—the run.

CHAPTER 7

Running and Jibing

Board and sail adjustment

RUNNING BEFORE THE WIND is a Laser's most demanding point of sail in terms of balance and concentration. If the wind is light, you must concentrate on catching each little puff and on keeping the boat moving at all times. If the wind is heavy, you must concentrate on keeping the boat upright by simultaneously shifting your weight and trimming the sail. Under these conditions this experience can be very thrilling because of the boat's speed and the sensation that you are on the brink of disaster.

For this downwind leg of the course, the Cunningham should be loose, except in strong winds when it should be just tight enough to remove wrinkles in the luff. The outhaul should be left as is. It is not necessary to make the sail fuller by easing the outhaul while running since the wind is simply pushing against the sail. Therefore the more area presented for the wind to act upon, the more effective the sail will be.

The traveler should also be left as is. It makes no differ-

John Rousmaniere
Tillman makes adjustments after rounding the windward mark. He will ease the Cunningham and raise the centerboard some more, but the traveler, vang, and outhaul will remain
tight.

ence whether it is in or out. In high winds, it is better to leave it tight so that when you round the leeward mark it will be properly adjusted for the beat. Occasionally the Brummel hooks connecting the sheet and traveler blocks will become twisted. If this happens it is possible for the traveler block to sheer off. This problem can be overcome by wrapping tape or placing a plastic tube around the Brummel hooks to keep them straight.

The "death roll"

When sailing downwind, particularly in heavy air, any small boat is susceptible to the "death roll"—violent rolling—and may capsize to windward. To prevent this you need to sheet in when you sense that the boat is going to roll to windward. This will apply force in the leeward direction and keep you from capsizing to windward. If you have weather helm or if the boat tends to heel to leeward, you need to ease the sheet. Never cleat the mainsheet when running. Instead, alternately sheet it in and out to keep the boat from rolling.

The sheet should be let all the way out in light and moderate air and trimmed somewhat in fresh air. Get in the habit of tying a tight figure-eight knot at the end of the sheet so it does not accidentally slip through the blocks.

The vang is an extremely important control. In a drifter it should be loose; in strong winds it should usually be as tight as you can get it. In between these extremes it should be tightened as the wind increases, loosened as it decreases. Since most sailing is done in the "in-between" conditions, the vang should be set up to keep the leech of the sail straight but not so tight that it hooks in or so loose that it falls off. The best way to keep the boat under control in strong winds is to tighten the vang to induce a bend in the boom. This will hold the sail relatively flat in a lateral plane and will help prevent the "death roll."

The centerboard will create the least amount of drag if it is most of the way up. However, it is both undesirable and

Carl Van Duyne

Heavy air and downwind sailing can present problems and special challenges. Here a
skipper struggles for control.

dangerous to remove it completely. It is undesirable because the water sloshing around in an empty trunk creates unwanted drag. It is dangerous because it reduces maneuverability to about zero and because it is possible to lose the board overboard. When sailing dead downwind, the top of the board should be just below the level of the boom so that you can jibe without having to lower the board. In this position there will be about two inches of board in the water below the boat. If you are sailing a course not quite downwind, you will want to have four to six inches of the board sticking in the water anyway. For better control, you should jibe with the board halfway down, particularly in heavier air. The importance of the additional board is the increased maneuverability resulting from greater lateral stability.

Always leave the rudder in the down position for safety and maneuverability. Raising the rudder will induce weather helm and destroy its hydrodynamic effectiveness.

On the run, fore-and-aft body position should be the same as for reaching. However, your weight by necessity will be closer inboard near the centerline of the boat. The Laser is forgiving as long as you are willing to move your weight rapidly to avoid excessive heeling. Always face forward with one hand on the sheet and the other on the tiller or hiking stick.

Jibing

In a strong wind a jibe can be a thrilling maneuver, and a safe one if done properly. The key to executing successful jibes lies in a combination of sailing by the lee and moving your weight. Assume you are running on starboard tack and wish to jibe onto port. You are sitting on the starboard edge of the cockpit facing forward. Lower the board to a halfway position. If the sheet is all the way out, bring it in about two feet and slowly bring the tiller toward you to bear off. Concentrate on keeping the boat absolutely flat. Move toward the center of the boat or even to the leeward side if necessary to keep the boat level, since you will now be sailing by the lee with the wind coming over the port quarter. When the sail is nearly ready to jibe, give the sheet a quick jerk with your right hand to start the boom across and to keep the sheet from catching on the transom corner. As the boom swings across, duck, slide to port, and *quickly* return the tiller to amidships or beyond to bring the boat back to a downwind course. Simultaneously change hands on the sheet and hiking stick. You are now sitting on the port edge of the cockpit and running on the port tack. Now raise your board again to the correct running position. (Another method is to switch tiller hands before the jibe, steering behind your back before moving across the cockpit.)

(A)

(B)

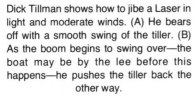

Dick Tillman shows how to jibe a Laser in light and moderate winds. (A) He bears off with a smooth swing of the tiller. (B) As the boom begins to swing over—the boat may be by the lee before this happens—he pushes the tiller back the other way.

John Rousmaniere

(C & D) When the jibe is completed, the boat is on a dead
run. Hands are switched on
the tiller and mainsheet as the
helmsman moves his weight to
the new windward side.

John Rousmaniere

(C)

(D)

The mainsheet may catch on the boat's transom during a jibe. The solution is a quick jerk on the sheet as the boom swings over, taking the slack out of the line.

For heavier helmsmen, or for anyone in light air, it is also possible to jibe by facing aft, grabbing the two parts of the sheet near the transom, and pulling the sail across. In this case, you face the stern and remain near the center of the boat. Steer the

John Weber

This skipper needs to get the boat flat before attempting to jibe.

boat dead downwind or slightly by the lee as you reach for the sheets to pull the sail across.

When jibing from one reach to another you must ease the main as you bear off before jibing. You normally approach the reaching mark on a beam reach. If it is windy and you try to jibe around the mark without letting the main out, you will very likely not be able to bear off at all. The boat will want to round up into the wind and the rudder will stall out and be ineffective when you try to bear away. So you must ease the main and keep the boat level as you turn to round the mark. Only when you are turned directly downwind, do you execute the jibe described here. If the course to the next mark is another reach you should then sheet in to the proper trim. Again, the board should be about halfway down for this maneuver, particularly in a breeze.

The art of jibing smoothly with speed and finesse comes only with practice. Anyone can jibe in moderate winds and smooth water. The only real way to learn how to handle the boat well and to jibe well is to go sailing on a windy day and risk a capsize or two. Experience is the best teacher, but only after the technique is completely understood.

CHAPTER 8

Practice

Individual practice

"PRACTICE MAKES PERFECT." Unfortunately, to all but the totally dedicated athlete, practice is often a monotonous but necessary way to maintain a certain degree of proficiency. However to a serious sailor, practice can be fun and challenging. One way to practice is by yourself, but that is not much fun and you lose the benefit of head to head competition.

However, one benefit in sailing alone is learning how to handle the boat. Practice tacking and jibing. Develop a smooth procedure and through constant repetition, learn to execute either maneuver without a thought. These two maneuvers are basic, and you should feel like a part of the boat in performing them. The boat will feel "right" when you have done it well and it will be equally obvious if you have done it wrong.

The more windy it is, the more valuable the practice will be. I remember watching one of the top French Finn sailors practicing on Lake Lucerne in Switzerland. The committee had cancelled a race because of a *Foehn* (a strong, treacherous, shift-

ing wind blowing between the steep mountains that surround
Lake Lucerne). But the Frenchman was out practicing one jibe
after another. Naturally, he turned over a few times, but he got
more practice under these conditions in 15 minutes than many
sailors get in a year. He loved every minute of it too, because he
knew the rest of us were watching from shore!

Boat against boat

A good way to practice and the most efficient way to develop
speed while sailing to windward is to sail alongside another boat
and match her in speed. Get as close as possible without interfering with each other's wind. When going to windward, the
skipper of the leeward boat becomes a "constant," sailing as fast
as possible but making no adjustments to his sail. The skipper
of the windward boat can then make changes in the various
controls, one at a time, to observe the effect on his speed in
relation to the leeward boat. Once he determines what makes
his boat go fast, he shares this knowledge with his partner and
the two change positions. The "constant" becomes the "exper-
imenter" and vice versa. In this manner each can quickly learn
what makes his boat go faster.

Informal racing

The best way to get all-around practice is to race. We used to
have a lot of fun doing this in Charleston. During the winter, a
half dozen "super racers" met each Sunday. We set up our own
courses using the government buoys in the river and either
started ourselves or used a volunteer committee boat. Most
times, however, we started informally by establishing a line that
was square to the wind, using a buoy at one end and a point on
land at the other. We all had watches and one of us would give a
two-minute verbal signal on which the others would key. We

used a two-minute starting sequence to speed up the races, and we sailed five or six short races in an afternoon. Each skipper was on his own to make sure that he was not over the imaginary line at the start. For the remainder of the course we selected other buoys in the river. If you do not have permanent marks

Hans Loffel

Match racing makes excellent practice and can be challenging for both participants whether beginner or expert.

in your racing area, it is fairly easy to construct some. The buoys do not have to be large because the entire course need only be one or two miles long and even a Clorox or a plastic milk bottle can be seen easily on a short course.

The better your competition, the better the practice. One way we increased the degree of competition was to have the lead boat re-round any mark at which she had a lead of two boat lengths or more. This made the racing closer and more interesting for everyone, and it gave the leader practice in rounding marks. If you do not have a permanent course or do not have time to place your own marks, then you can start yourselves simply by lining up so that no one has an advantage.

This method of starting gives the racers another opportunity to equalize the competition. You can give either the windward or leeward boats an advantage over the others. Thus, for the start of the second race you can reverse the order of finish and position the boats so that the first boat is in the least advantageous position, the second boat in the next position, and so on. This method is good and it can be easily controlled for two to five boats.

For more than five boats, there is a version of the informal start described here known as the rabbit or gate start, in which the wake of a boat on one tack is the starting line for everybody on the other tack. This requires more skill and practice than the informal start but for a larger group of boats it is effective and fair. It does not put anyone in a disadvantageous position.

The "rabbit" is the boat which crosses the fleet, on port tack, hard on the wind, and during this time she has complete right of way. The rest of the boats start on starboard tack by ducking under the stern of the "rabbit." After all the boats have passed astern of the "rabbit," the "rabbit" tacks and, if there has not been a major wind shift, all boats will be on an even line. The race then continues, maximizing the opportunity for each sailor to use strategy, boat handling, tactics, and rules to his advantage.

In the more formal version occasionally used at large re-

Carl Van Duyne

St. Francis YC in San Francisco sponsored a slalom race for champions in 1974. Note reefed sails.

gattas, the lead or "rabbit" boat is followed closely by a guard or committee boat and sails past a set mark closehauled on port tack. The "gate" is then formed between the committee boat and the set mark through which the rest of the fleet starts on starboard on a given signal. After a predetermined time or when the fleet has crossed the line, the rabbit may jibe onto starboard around the committee boat and start racing.

The slalom course

Another good way to practice is to sail a slalom course, either alone or against competition. It requires the skipper to tack and jibe at frequent intervals and test his boat-handling ability.

The course consists of a number of buoys and a "sail" to

keep the buoys evenly spaced and in line with the wind. The object is to start at the downwind buoy (the "sail") and tack upwind, between the buoys. After rounding the buoy farthest to windward you then jibe downwind between the buoys. This forced tacking and jibing to complete the course is challenging and exciting, particularly under breezy or high-wave conditions.

Competition can be introduced by constructing two courses and laying them side by side. In this way, two boats can be given timed starts or start evenly from a dead luffing standstill. Whichever one negotiates all the buoys in the least amount of time is the winner.

An eight-buoy course will give excellent training and is simple and inexpensive (under $5) to construct. Here is a list of the materials needed and instructions on how to make one:

Seven one-gallon plastic milk bottles with caps
One plastic trash or leaf bag
Eight two-foot lengths of porch-swing-type chain
Eight three-foot lengths of nylon twine
One spool of nylon twine (at least 300 feet long)
One two-foot length of broom handle
One-five-pound weight

To each bottle handle, tie a three-foot length of twine followed by a two-foot length of chain or comparable weight. Stuff the twine and chain into the bottle for storage and replace the cap. Unroll the nylon twine and tie a three-inch loop at the beginning and every 36 feet until you have eight loops on a 252-foot length of twine. Wind the twine onto the broom handle. (*Hint:* a finishing nail pounded into the end of the broom handle and placed in the chuck of a hand drill makes an efficient winding device.) Take the plastic trash bag and blow it full of air by mouth or bicycle pump. Close it with several wraps of twine to make it airtight. Attach a length of twine and chain to it also. Now you are ready to go to the sailing area to lay the course.

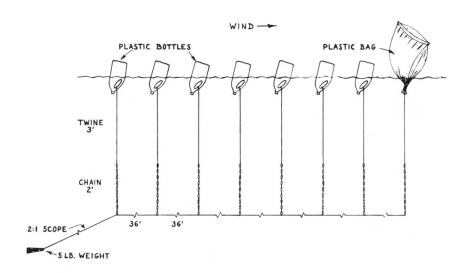

Jack Smith drawing

A slalom course offers an interesting and effective way to practice tacking and jibing.

At the course site, drop the five-pound weight (bricks tied together, hunk of lead, mushroom anchor, etc.) into the water with a 2:1 scope. Tie the end to the twine on the broom handle. Drift or proceed downwind, letting the twine unwind from the broom handle. Each time a loop appears, pass the loop through the next-to-the-last link of chain on a bottle and then pass the last link of chain through the loop to secure it. (This makes it unnecessary to tie and untie any knots.) Tie the plastic trash bag to the last loop at the end of the 252 feet of twine. This acts as a "sail" and keeps the bottles evenly spaced and in line with the wind. The lengths of chain keep the 252 feet of linking twine submerged so that the boats may pass over it.

To pick up the course, untie the trash bag and wind up the line, removing the plastic bottles one by one. The bottles can then be compactly stored by replacing the line and chain in them and sliding them onto the broom handle.

Practice is the one element which is essential to improve one's racing ability. This chapter has discussed several interesting and challenging methods, including individual practice, boat against boat, informal racing, rabbit starts, and the slalom course. Practicing in these ways is fun and gives everyone a chance to identify weaknesses and to work to correct them.

Go-Fast Techniques

A competitive edge

ANYONE WHO HAS RACED knows that there are special adjustments and techniques associated with each particular racing
class that give a sailor an edge on the competition. Here are
some advanced adjustments and techniques, not yet discussed,
which I feel are important to winning in a Laser.

Starting

There are certain critical places in a race that normally determine the final outcome or, at the least, have a big effect on it.
By far, the most significant is the start. The boat that gets the
best start will almost always win. This law varies directly with
the level of competition; that is, the lower the level of competition, the easier it is to win after getting a good start. Conversely,
the better the competition, the more important a super start is
to placing among the top. A good start puts you ahead of the

competition. It allows you to pick your side of the course, tack freely, and get the wind shifts first. A good example of this occurred in the last race of the 1973 Laser North American Championship in San Diego, California. The race committee had imposed a "30-second rule" for the start. This meant that any boat over the line during the last 30-second countdown would be disqualified. Any disqualification would remain in effect even after a general recall. This rule effectively kept even the most anxious starter honest. The race started and Ward McKimm, a partner of Ian Bruce's at Performance Sailcraft, was first to the weather mark. He held a slim lead throughout the race. However, he did not win because he had been one foot over the starting line. That foot both won and lost him the race. Becoming expert in this one area alone will almost guarantee your becoming a winner.

An accurate and readable stopwatch is a must for getting a good start. A wrist type is better than one worn around the neck, since you have the use of both hands and there is no danger of getting the watch caught on the sheet. It should be large enough to read easily even when it is covered with spray. Don't forget to wind it, and remember what starting interval you are using.

The compass

Most Laser racing is on small bodies of water where the shore line can be used to check changes in headings due to windshifts. Under these circumstances a compass is not necessary. If you race in open water, however, a good compass with easy to read numbers can be useful. It can be permanently mounted on the deck or temporarily secured so it can be removed later for use on other boats. Class rules permit only one compass, and it may not be recessed in the deck.

Since most dinghy races are short and include many boats, you can normally identify wind shifts effectively by observing the headings of those boats around you. For example, if you are 50 feet directly ahead of another boat and notice that she is gradually swinging to leeward of your wake, it is likely that you have both been headed. If the other boat tacks, you should, too. Under the same circumstances, if you were the leeward boat, a tack would again be in order.

Remember that a compass should be used, like a masthead fly, only as an assist or as an additional source of information. Do not simply glue your eyes to it and be oblivious to everything else. It takes practice and experience to use a compass effectively, and it is not necessary to have one to win.

Roll tacking

Here is a technique of tacking which many expert sailors use in round-bottomed dinghies in light to moderate wind. It creates increased lift in the sail during the tacking maneuver and results in a smoother, faster tack. It is used primarily in light to medium winds. In a Laser it works as follows: just prior to the tack, heel the boat to windward by hiking harder. As the boat heels to windward, push the helm down and tack. When the boat passes head to wind and as the rail under you touches the water, quickly move to the opposite side and complete the tack. This maneuver requires a great deal of practice; once it is perfected, you will find yourself gaining nearly a boat length on your non-roll-tacking competitors each time you tack.

Hanging in

In a strong wind, it is not unusual to go out of control. At first you may feel that the boat is tender and unforgiving. However, if you practice and are determined, you will find that you can generally save her from going over. Once you have learned how far the boat can go without flipping, you will save valuable time in a race. If a blast knocks you down on the beat, hike hard. The sail may be parallel to the water, but by bending far back over the water you can usually avoid a capsize. On a run, where capsizes normally occur to windward, the key is to push the helm to leeward and to get your weight over the leeward rail, which by now is rolling up in the air. As long as you can keep the helm and your weight to leeward, you can save her even when the mast is nearly parallel to the water. Lean over the high side and keep hold of the hiking stick. If all else fails, let go of the sheet and the tiller and use all your energy, weight, and concentration to balance the boat.

Capsizing

To get the most speed on a downwind leg you are often on the brink of capsizing. Even the best sailors may dump under extreme wind and wave conditions. The quicker you get the boat up and underway again the better off you are. The normal procedure to right the boat quickly is to stand on the end of the board and crawl into the boat as she rights. However, in the case of capsizing to windward, the wind will get under the sail and lift it so quickly that the boat will capsize the opposite way, on top of you, before you can crawl in to counterbalance it. This necessitates a swim under or around the boat to right her again, a time consuming maneuver in either case. Whenever and however you capsize, righting the boat will always be easier when the bow is pointed into the wind.

Here is a sophisticated boat-righting technique when the boat has capsized to windward. Stand or, preferably, pull down on the board to right the boat. As the boat comes up, wrap yourself around the board and ride it under the water. As the boat continues to come up, while you are under the water, maneuver yourself onto the opposite side of the board. As the boat starts to capsize in the opposite direction, you will already be on the board and your weight will stop the second roll to leeward. You can quickly recover and get underway. This

Hang in there!

John Weber

This skipper is climbing onto the centerboard to right his boat after having turned turtle.

Ellie Martin

technique requires a little practice to perfect but will get you up and going quickly. Remember to wear your life jacket.

Sail controls

Cunningham. Although the start is the single most important part of the race, there are many little things which, added together, become significant. One of these is how the Cunningham is rigged. Tie the end to the gooseneck fitting and feed the line through the grommet from the port side so that it comes directly down to the deck along the starboard side of the gooseneck. Then when you are approaching the start on the starboard tack, you will be able to make more precise last minute adjustments in the Cunningham because the boom, being to port, will not interfere with the line.

If it is necessary to tighten the Cunningham while beating under puffy or windy conditions, a good technique is to luff up slightly, hiking extra hard as you do so, then reach in to tighten the Cunningham. Bear off to close hauled as soon as the adjustment is made. Although you will lose some speed because the boat was heeling, you will work to weather sufficiently during this maneuver to offset the difference. It is within the class rules to rig a purchase.

Vang. Sailors weighing over 200 pounds should try easing the vang slightly on marginal planing reaches. This will produce a fuller sail with more power. Easing the vang even more should assist light weight sailors in a blow since a loose leech will spill wind, ease weather helm, and help keep the boom from dragging in the water (thus averting possible capsizes). Reversing the blocks of the vang (the jamming block on the boom and the fiddle block on the mast) makes it easier to adjust. The pull is down and more convenient to the cockpit.

Outhaul. Perhaps the most critical adjustment is the outhaul. If the foot of the sail is too flat and tight, you lose power. If it is too full and loose, you cannot point. Learn to adjust the outhaul while racing. A technique for doing this while beating is to ease the sheet a foot or two, place your foot on the leeward edge of the cockpit so you can hold the tiller steady with your leg, then lean toward the boom and grasp the outhaul at a point midway between the end of the boom and the cleat. Pull it toward you and take up the slack through the cleat with the other hand. With practice you can adjust the outhaul without a significant loss of speed. So far, I have seen few Laser racers easing the outhaul for the reaches, although this may be a technique which will prove itself in the future. Nevertheless, it is not unusual for the wind to change strength during the course of the race and in this case the proper outhaul adjustment will significantly affect the speed of the boat. It is highly recommended that the clew be rigged with a purchase, particularly if you wish to adjust underway.

Humming boards and rudders

Some centerboards and rudders hum under planing conditions. This may be music to some ears but it is an unwanted nuisance to others. Most sailors want to eliminate hum since theory has it that the vibrations absorb energy that might otherwise propell the boat. Those wishing to eliminate this irritating and energy robbing vibration might consider the following suggestions.

Measure the trailing edge widths of the centerboard and the rudder. They should be tapered to $1/16$ inch with a square trailing edge so that the water passing by will leave cleanly. George Moffat writes in Stuart Walker's book, *Performance Advances in Small Boat Racing*, that a squared trailing edge about $1/16$-inch thick is as efficient as a knife sharp edge. A thick or rounded edge will cause high drag.

You should also check to see that the underwater surfaces are true and symmetrical with the centerline of the boat. It is equally important that they be relatively smooth.

Bermuda News Bureau, Eric Johnson

When conditions permit, experiment with shifting your weight and pumping the sheet to
ride the waves and promote or initiate planing.

Mainsheet

For competitive racing, the mainsheet should be 40 to 42 feet long. Standard sheets provided with the boats are often shorter than this. A long sheet gives you an advantage on the run since the sail is more efficient when the boom is perpendicular to the boat or beyond. It also allows you to sail by the lee, which is sometimes tactically wise. There is one danger to be aware of, however: the further out the boom goes, the more likely you are to capsize to weather. The top of the sail creates lift at right angles to the boat in the weather direction when allowed to twist off in front of the mast. When jibing, or if caught in a puff, be quick to sheet in and balance the boat. In windy or puffy conditions, when it is risky to let the sail all the way out, the conservative sailor will put a knot about ten feet from the end of the sheet.

Pumping and ooching

In wind permitting wave surfing or, of course, in heavy air, the best downwind sailors are always moving in their boats. You will see them shifting their weight forward and aft—sometimes violently—as they ride waves. They will also trim and ease the sheet sharply. Moving the crew's weight around is called "ooching," and trimming and easing the sheet sharply and repeatedly is called "pumping."

According to Appendix Two of the International Yacht Racing Union's 1973 edition of the Racing Rules, both are legal if used to *promote* or initiate planing or surfing down waves. You may not pump or ooch in order to *maintain* a plane or a surf. The rules say this about pumping: "Once a boat has started surfing or planing on a particular set of wave forms, from then on she must let the natural action of wind and water propel her without further *rapid* trimming and releasing of the sails."

The idea is to prohibit "fanning" the boat around the

course. If you are protested, you will have to be able to prove that surfing or planing conditions existed when you were pumping or ooching. Rocking, or persistently rolling the boat from side to side, is also prohibited. In drifting conditions, rocking a Laser will push her through the water at a surprisingly rapid rate. It will help you get home from an abandoned race, but you may not rock during the race.

Fixing a leak

It is unusual for Lasers to leak. However, a drain plug is built in for this eventuality. From the racing standpoint, it is important that the hull be dry, since water only makes the boat heavier. Get in the habit of draining the boat if you find water entering the hull. More often than not, water finds its way into the hull when it is upside down in outside storage. Sometimes the sheer (the junction of the hull and the deck) will have a pin-sized opening, or the centerboard trunk or cockpit drain plug may not be entirely sealed. If you find that the hull is dry under nonplaning conditions but that it has leaked under planing conditions, the sheer on top of the centerboard trunk would be a suspect area. To detect a leak, turn the boat upside down, put a soapy solution at the sheer or in the centerboard trunk and have someone blow into the drain hole (or use a vacuum cleaner in reverse). Any leaks can be easily identified by the resulting bubbles. After the leaks are located, a marine sealer used as directed will solve the problem.

CHAPTER 10

Physical Fitness

The importance of being in shape

YOU SHOULD BE IN GOOD PHYSICAL CONDITION to sail a Laser effectively even in medium winds. Being in good shape is most important going upwind, when the boat must be kept flat and driven hard. The helmsman must give long term, maximum effort under these conditions. On a short course, hiking is done in a flat-out position, insteps under the straps (which should be tight), legs as far out on the rail as possible, and body nearly horizontal over the water. You should just be able to see the tips of your toes.

On a longer course it is impossible to hike continuously this way. Instead, you should position your weight as far outboard as possible and hike in a drooping or hooked position. This means keeping your knees bent, putting your seat over the sheer, and sitting in a practically upright position. You should be able to hold this position for up to ten minutes at a time. If this does not seem very long, try it sometime.

79

Sail a lot

Naturally, you must have a program to get yourself in this type of condition. The best way to get into shape is to sail. Continuous practice in medium and heavy air will strengthen the ankle, shin, thigh, and stomach muscles which are so important for long-term hiking. Continuous practice will also toughen hands and strengthen arm muscles for the constant attention to sail adjustments required both on and off the wind. Continuous practice will condition the body in general for the exhausting efforts often required on a tough, five-race weekend series.

If the weather and circumstances are not conducive to continuous practice, a physical conditioning plan of off-the-water exercises must be developed and practiced on a regular basis. The plan should be specifically designed to strengthen arm, thigh, and stomach muscles, toughen hands, and improve cardiovascular condition. Calisthenics, weight lifting, and use of a hiking bench will improve muscle tone, running or skipping will improve cardiovascular condition.

As a minimum, I do sit-ups and push-ups at home. Regular workouts with weights to augment this drill would be better, using routines to exercise and strengthen the muscles used in sailing.

The hiking bench

Before a major regatta, I work out on a hiking bench. It is a simple homemade bench which simulates hiking in a Laser. The seat is the same width as the deck, the hiking strap is the same height as the one in the cockpit, and the sheeting arrangement is similar to the Laser's. The hiking bench can be made in two hours using materials that cost less than $5.

To use it, attach twin sheets led through the eyes to pulleys, attached to the eaves of the garage or house, or perhaps to a joist in the basement. The ends of the sheets are secured to

Dick Tillman works out on his hiking bench which he built in a few hours.

Linda Tillman

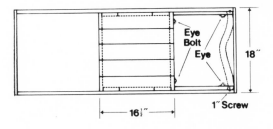

PARTS LIST		
Material	Length	Number
1 x 4	48″	2
1 x 4	29	2
1 x 4	18	6
1 x 4	16½	5
1 x 4	14	4
1 x 4	11	2
2″ webbing	24	1
screws	1	6
nails	1¼ – 1½	4 doz.
pad eye		2
eye bolt	¼ x 2	2

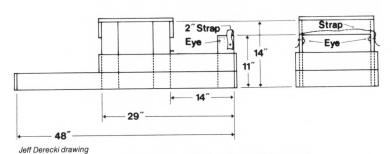

Jeff Derecki drawing

Plans and parts list for a Laser hiking bench.

suitable weights, such as a bucketful of sand or water, or to some heavy shockcord. Some vigorous pumping on a sheet hauling a pail of water weighing approximately 25 pounds should be more than enough to raise a few blisters.

As a training program I recommend that you start working on the bench at least two weeks before a regatta. Exercise about

A Dutch sailor hikes during a heavy-air close reach. Note the extra-long tiller extension, the numbered tape on the board, and the tight outhaul, vang, and Cunningham. Instead of cleating the sheet, which is led through an Elvstrom ratchet block, he snubs it by leading it over his leg.

Adriaan Pels

a half hour a day, every other day. Hike as long and as hard as you can and pump the sheet ten or 12 times, alternating hands. Rest days will give your hands a chance to toughen up and your leg and stomach muscles time to rebuild.

It is quite possible to be out of breath and nearly exhausted at the end of a long reach or run in heavy air and rough seas in the Laser. Running and skipping rope are two very good exercises to improve your cardiovascular condition. A regular program of running will do much to give you the stamina to stay with it. I try to run a mile every day for a month or so before a regatta.

You will find that in competition, the harder you work, the better you will do. The leaders will be hiking harder and longer than the followers.

CHAPTER 11

Transporting the Laser

Getting around

BESIDES BEING A SIMPLE BOAT TO SAIL, the Laser is easy to transport. There are two basic ways to carry a Laser—by trailer or car top. Trailing is undoubtedly easier for short distances, i.e., from your house to the lake or beach. Cartopping is better for longer hauls.

Trailing

If you do use a trailer it can be a small one because the boat is lightweight. You should be especially careful to support the boat at the mast step and at the drain hole at the after end of the cockpit—the two points where the boat is strongest—so that the bottom or deck (depending on whether the boat is upside down or right side up) does not deflect. It is easy to deform the boat with poor-fitting cradles. If the trailer has fore-and-aft running pads, they should be located at the turn of the bilge,

John Rousmaniere

As long as boats are properly supported, you can load up like this for a regatta. Most sailors just tie their boats to padded roof or luggage racks and lash their spars alongside.

where the bottom curves into the topsides. As an alternative, the cradles could run perpendicular to the keel and conform perfectly to the boat's bottom. The boat should be tied down securely with two straps. The rudder, tiller, and centerboard should be carried in the car, wrapped in a padded cover to protect them from being nicked and scraped.

Any fiberglass boat left sitting on improper supports can be temporarily or even permanently deformed. Check frequently to make sure your boat is resting properly on its cradles. I have seen several hulls pushed in by poor-fitting cradles or from being tied down too tightly. In most cases, the bottoms return to their normal shape after the boats have been turned onto their decks and left upside down for a few days. A serious dent, which affects the shape of the Airex core in the hull, will leave you with permanent damage.

Graham Hall

A ten-boat Laser rig transports this fleet between regattas on the West Coast. Two have been unloaded from the sides and one from the top.

Cartopping

When you are cartopping there is no trailer to worry about, and driving and parking are both a lot easier. You can go faster too, since many areas have a limited speed for vehicles pulling trailers. A few years back, when the Finn Nationals were at Huntington Lake in California, I tried to explain to the police that I was pulling a boat, not a trailer, and could therefore go faster than the 55 mph limit. They were not convinced. No wonder many California sailors cartop their small dinghies!

The best way to cartop a Laser is with the boat upside down, bow forward. This position offers the least wind resistance and centers the boat fairly far forward over the car. Any one of the standard roof racks is suitable since the load is minimal. The racks should be placed under the mast hole and under the after end of the cockpit. Some skippers put the boat on top of the roof with only a piece of Styrofoam or rug padding to protect the car. You can easily travel along at an economical (and legal) 55 mph, but it is a good idea to lash the boat to the rear door handles or bumpers rather than to completely trust the roof racks. The spars will fit nicely alongside the hull or on top of the boat.

It is equally easy to cartop two Lasers. Put the second one directly over the first, both in a deck down, bow forward position. Three boat cushions are sufficient padding between the boats but each boat should be tied to the car separately.

CHAPTER 12

What to Wear

Warm and cold weather

A little thought about what to wear while sailing a Laser can be crucial, both to enjoying the boat and to winning races. The two major considerations are (1) keeping cool and protected from the sun in summer, and (2) keeping warm and dry in cold water or cold air.

On most hot days, a swimming suit or a pair of shorts will be adequate, although a pair of sweatpants can make hiking more comfortable and will protect the knees and shins. For anyone who tends to burn easily, a long sleeved shirt with collar and a good sun hat are musts. Zinc oxide ointment will protect your nose. Nothing is worse than starting off the second day of a regatta with a bad sunburn. Shoes are not necessary. This is one boat where sailing barefoot is all right, although you should watch out for sunburn on your insteps. Air conditioner tubing placed over the hiking straps will keep the straps from cutting into your feet.

Cold weather sailing can be enjoyable providing you are

comfortable. When the temperature drops to 60 degrees, a satisfactory outfit to wear is a pair of sweatpants with chest high foul weather pants. A pair of high sea boots will keep your feet warm and dry even when there is water in the cockpit. The foul weather pants, pulled over the tops of the boots, will effectively keep spray out. A good, heavy wool sweater with a foul weather top over it will keep the rest of you warm and dry. So will a good parka.

If the water temperature is low, a wet suit is a life saver. The 1973 Midwinter Championship in Miami was hit by a freak storm that brought 40-degree weather to Miami and snow as far south as Jacksonville. Many of us were caught unprepared, without wet suits. Believe me, it was cold! In the coldest climates a full wet suit is worthwhile, although it can be bulky. In most cases however, a short wet suit is satisfactory. I have one which comes midway down my thighs. The arms are cut off at the shoulder to allow complete freedom of movement. It keeps the trunk of the body warm and, with the exertion required to sail a race, has always kept me warm.

Life jackets

Every sailor should be in the habit of wearing a well-designed, safe, life jacket. The only time I feel secure in not wearing one is on a hot day in a drifter. A life jacket does no good lying loose in the cockpit when the wind suddenly kicks up and your hands are busy enough keeping the boat upright, without trying to get a life jacket on as well. I would recommend a jacket which has proper government or sailing authority approval.

What to take to a regatta

Thought and preparation regarding what to wear while sailing a Laser can be just as important to winning as any other single

John Weber   John Rousmaniere

In cold, blowy weather, there is no
substitute for staying warm and dry,
as the sailor above is dressed to do. A
well-designed life jacket is an abso-
lute must and every sailor should be
in the habit of wearing one.

Bermuda News Bureau, Eric Johnson

aspect of the race. Here is a list of clothing that I take to regattas as well as a checklist of equipment for my boat.

Equipment	Quantity
Life jacket	1
Swimming suit/shorts	2
Wet suit (full or short)	1
Sweatpants/dungarees	2
Long sleeved shirt with collar	2
Wool cap	1
Sun hat	1
Foul weather suit (top and pants)	1
Wool sweater	2
Wool socks	2 pair
Cotton socks	2 pair
Boat shoes	1 pair
Sea boots (or wet suit boots)	1 pair
Towels	2
Sunglasses	2 pair
Sailing gloves	1 pair
Stop watch	1
Wet or dry #400	2
#600	2
Liquid soap and sponge	1 each
Drinking water container	1

CHAPTER 13

Sportsmanship

Fair and friendly competition

SINCE SO MUCH OF THIS BOOK HAS DEALT WITH RACING, it seems proper to conclude with a comment about sportsmanship. In my opinion, racing small boats is the ultimate combination of mental and physical skills. Sailors seek an ever-increasing level of competition and derive tremendous satisfaction when they are able to beat those whom they consider better than themselves. The greatest satisfaction goes to those who win fairly and squarely. It is much better to win by sailing faster than by altering the boat unfairly or by registering a questionable protest. Winning by using a standard boat with standard equipment is better than outspending and "out-gadgeting" the competition. With the Laser there is no choice, since only the compass, the mainsheet ratchet and cleat, or centerlead swivel, and the telltale are optional.

Everyone enjoys friendly rather than cutthroat competition. The spirit of sportsmanship should always prevail. I remember vividly a few examples which illustrate this spirit.

In one race at the 1959 Snipe World Championship I was caught on the starting line on port tack in light air, bobbing up and down with no way, when the gun fired. A competitor with good momentum was coming toward us on starboard tack. Rather than pinch up and tag us out, he bore off slightly and purposefully avoided us. The individual was Paul Elvstrom, who has won four Olympic gold medals and many world championships.

At the 1966 European Finn Championship I loaned an extra stopwatch to a Russian, Valentin Mankin. He repaid the favor two years later by loaning me his own mast when he observed that I had poor boat speed. His generosity and sportsmanlike attitude, crossing international and political boundaries, will always be appreciated. He has won two Olympic gold medals.

More recently, in a local Snipe regatta, we lost our whisker pole on a reach. We sailed the next run holding the jib out, and lost several places. With another race yet to go we were in poor spirits until a competitor offered us his spare pole. I am sure that he got as much or more satisfaction in the giving as we did in the receiving.

These are only three acts of sportsmanship I have witnessed. Other sailors can recall as many or more. The satisfaction in racing comes from doing your best, improving with practice, and helping each other enjoy close racing by clean and fair sailing. As far as a Laser is concerned, this means that each Laser owner should know the class rules, especially the preamble which stresses the one-design character of the Laser. The Laser was designed to determine the best racer among individuals, not boats. The rules begin with the statement that "any alteration of the hull form, construction, equipment, spars, sail or running rigging, as supplied by the builder, except as is specifically authorized by these Rules, is a breach of these Rules, not only in spirit but in substance, and is prohibited.

The class rules cannot cover every possibility concerning material changes to a Laser. The intent, however, is clear, and

Ellie Martin

Sailing her flat out.

the boat's one-design character will be protected at every level for the enjoyment of those who want a Laser for what it is.

Enjoy yourself

I have been racing small sailboats for many years. During this time, I have never lost enthusiasm for competitive racing and it is always fun to try and win. Still it is *more* fun to win, so I hope this book will help you sail Lasers faster and better, and through sportsmanship and fair sailing enjoy the sport to the fullest. Good luck.

Appendix 1:
The Laser

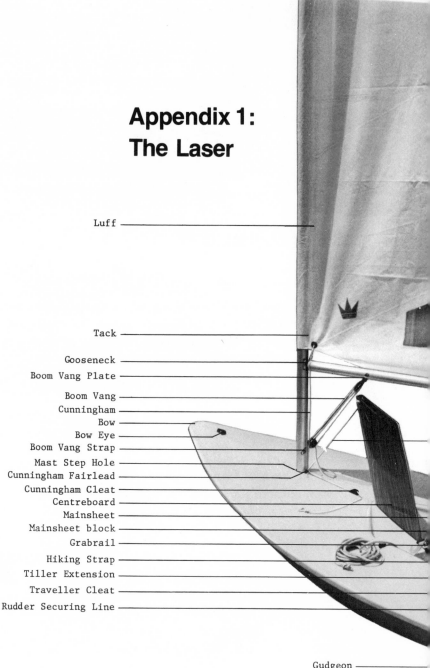

Luff

Tack

Gooseneck

Boom Vang Plate

Boom Vang

Cunningham

Bow

Bow Eye

Boom Vang Strap

Mast Step Hole

Cunningham Fairlead

Cunningham Cleat

Centreboard

Mainsheet

Mainsheet block

Grabrail

Hiking Strap

Tiller Extension

Traveller Cleat

Rudder Securing Line

Gudgeon

Rudder Stop

Pintle

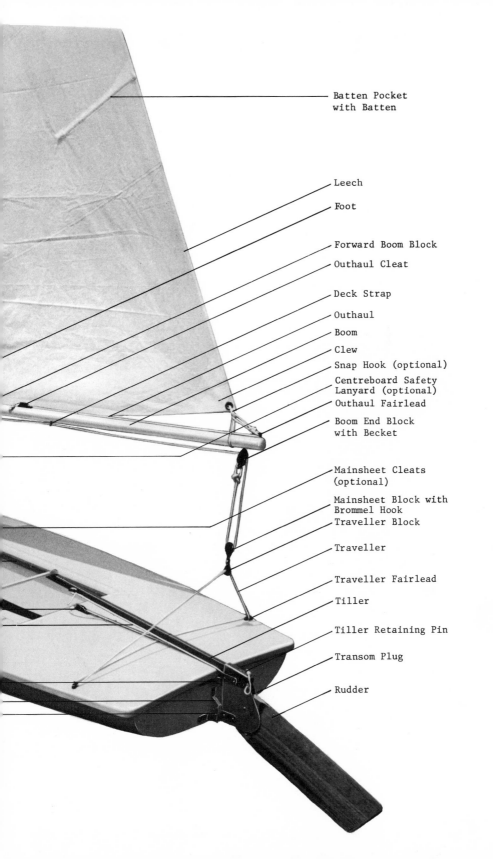

Batten Pocket
with Batten

Leech

Foot

Forward Boom Block

Outhaul Cleat

Deck Strap

Outhaul

Boom

Clew

Snap Hook (optional)

Centreboard Safety
Lanyard (optional)

Outhaul Fairlead

Boom End Block
with Becket

Mainsheet Cleats
(optional)

Mainsheet Block with
Brommel Hook

Traveller Block

Traveller

Traveller Fairlead

Tiller

Tiller Retaining Pin

Transom Plug

Rudder

Appendix 2:
Rigging your Laser

photographs, Hans Loffel

Set the boat with the bow pointing into the wind on a reasonably level spot near the water's edge. Check to see that the transom and cockpit drain plugs are in.

Assemble two-piece mast (Fig. 1) making sure that the smaller part of the gray collar is fully inserted into the large aluminum section.

Install the battens, pushing each batten firmly forward against the elastic, then sliding the rear end of the batten down, so that it sits well in the back of the pocket.

Fig. 1

Slide the sail over the mast (Fig. 2) making sure that there is no twist in the sleeve and that the Cunningham hole is on the same side as the gooseneck.

Make sure the mast hole is perfectly clean, since the mast must go all the way to the bottom. Furthermore, any sand, dirt, etc. in the mast step will cause wear and eventually damage the boat.

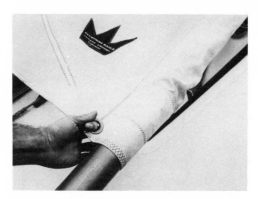

Fig. 2

97

Fig. 3

Set the complete mast and sail into the mast step and secure the Cunningham line (Fig. 3 and Fig. 4) which ensures that the mast stays in the boat. Tie a figure-eight knot in the end of the Cunningham line.

Place the boom on the gooseneck fitting.

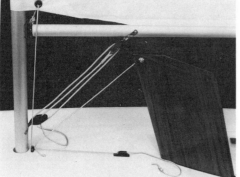

Fig. 4

The outhaul line should be deadended at the fairlead on the end of the boom, then taken through the clew of the sail and back through the outhaul fairlead, before being led forward to the outhaul cleat (Fig. 5). Tie a figure-eight knot in the end of the outhaul line. A short line tied through the clew and around the boom prevents the clew from rising.

Fig. 5

To provide a quick release of the sail
when coming on shore, or when docking,
or in an emergency, we recommend the
alternative rigging of a quick-release outhaul with a snap-hook, as shown in (Fig.
6).

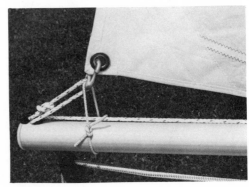

Fig. 6

Rig the mainsheet (Fig. 7), tying one end
to the becket on the boom end block. Be
sure to lead the sheet through the deck-
strap on the boom, through the forward
boom block and down to the mainsheet
block.

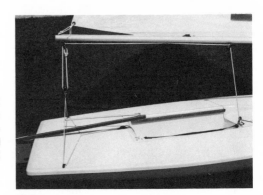

Fig. 7

Rig the boom vang (Fig. 8). The larger
fitting with the jamb cleat is attached to
the boom vang strap and the smaller fitting with the key to the boom vang plate.
Give the vang enough tension to keep
the boom from rising above a horizontal.
Increase tension as the wind blows
harder.

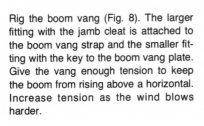
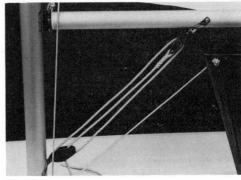

Fig. 8

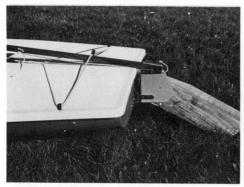

Fig. 9

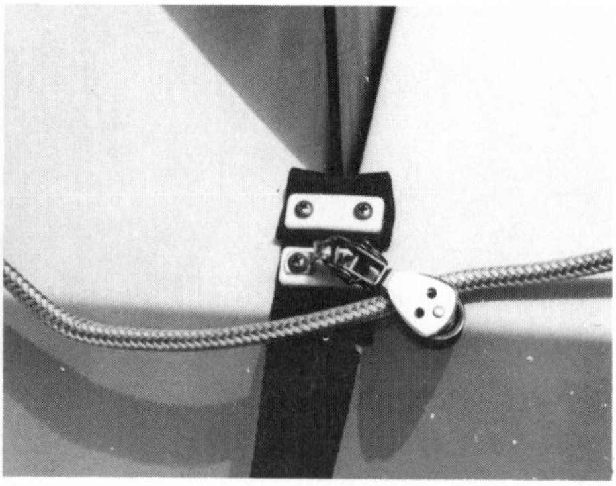

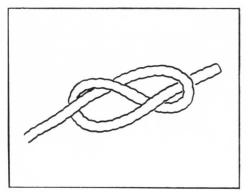

Fig. 10

Fig. 11

Set the boat near the edge of the water. Install the rudder (Fig. 9), making sure that the rudder stop prevents the lower pintle from riding up. Place the tiller through the traveller and into the rudder head, insert the tiller retaining pin. Pass the securing line once around the cleat; do not knot it. This is enough tension to hold the rudder down while sailing. The rudder will kick up automatically should you hit anything.

Launch the boat — with the bow still pointing into the wind. Install the centerboard. Check that the rubber stopper (Fig. 10) provides enough friction to hold the board in place without jamming it. Tension may be adjusted by tightening or loosening the screws which hold the rubber stopper.

To prevent the centerboard from falling out, should you capsize, it is advantageous to put a safety lanyard on it. A shock cord or combination of line and shock cord, attached to the upper forward edge of the board and fastened to the boom vang strap is authorized and recommended (Fig. 11).

Tie figure-eight knots in the ends of the mainsheet, Cunningham and outhaul lines to prevent their slipping out (Fig. 12).

Fig. 12

Appendix 3:
Further Reading

You should get into the habit of reading books and articles about sailboat racing. Frequently, the authors offer insights into techniques that you may not have considered.

Here are some books that you might find helpful. Remember that these represent one sailor's choice and that there are many more.

Stuart H. Walker, THE TACTICS OF SMALL BOAT RACING (*W.W. Norton Co., 1966*). A good study of racing tactics—so important in Laser competition where speed is frequently even.

Garry Hoyt, GO FOR THE GOLD (*Quadrangle Books/Yacht Racing Magazine, 1972*). A pointed, humorous book on tactics and psychology on the race course.

Richard Creagh-Osborne (ed.), ELVSTROM SPEAKS (*Quadrangle Books/One-Design and Offshore Yachtsman Magazine, 1970*). An autobiography of four-time Olympic gold medalist Paul Elvstrom, with many hints on racing small boats.

Larry Lewis, SAIL IT FLAT (*Quadrangle Books/One-Design and Offshore Yachtsman Magazine, 1971*). A brief but lively and informative book about racing Sunfish that is also helpful for sailors of other small dinghies.

Robert N. Bavier, Jr., THE NEW YACHT RACING RULES (*W.W. Norton & Co., 1973*). An analysis of the racing rules.

Bill Bentsen, THE YACHT RACING RULES TODAY (*Dodd, Mead & Co., 1974*). Newest of the rules books, this one puts each rule into its most frequent race-course situations and has a good discussion of the most basic rules.

You might also purchase the rules ($2.50) and the appeals ($3.00) from the United States Yacht Racing Union, 1133 Avenue of the Americas, New York, N.Y. 10036. In other countries, the rules are available from the sport's national authorities.

Appendix 4:
International Laser Class Association Constitution and Bylaws

CONSTITUTION

NAME
1. The name of the Association shall be the INTERNATIONAL LASER CLASS ASSOCIATION, with Head Office at 91 Hymus Boulevard, Pointe Claire, Quebec, Canada.

INSIGNIA
2. The emblem of the Class shall be the recognized Laser symbol; and the insignia of the officers shall be those prescribed by By-Law.

OBJECTS
3. The objects of the Association are
    (a) to provide a medium of exchange of information among Laser sailors throughout the world to enhance the enjoyment of these sailboats;
    (b) to promote and develop Laser class racing in all countries, under uniform rules; and
    (c) to encourage and foster the enjoyment of the sporting and recreational aspects of sailing.

POLICY
4. It shall be the policy of the Association to maintain the Laser as the epitome of a strict one-design class of sailboat.

JURISDICTION
5. The Association has authority over all activities of the Laser Class throughout the world, and its powers shall be vested in and carried

out by the World Council, Regional Executive Committees, District Associations and Fleets as provided in this Constitution and any By-Laws passed pursuant to the provisions hereof; all subject to and in accordance with the General Rules and By-Laws of the International Yacht Racing Union.

ORGANIZATION
World Council
6. (1) The Association shall be governed by the World Council comprised of the Chairman of each Regional Executive Committee from time to time holding office, the immediate Past President of the World Council, the Executive Secretary, the two appointed members of the Advisory Council, and such additional officers to be appointed by the Council for such term as it may from time to time determine.

(2) The World Council shall meet not less frequently than once per year and the first meeting shall take place within two months of the election of the Regional Chairmen. The time and location of meetings shall, if possible, coincide with the holding of a world or a regional championship meet.

(3) The World Council shall elect from amongst themselves the President and Vice-President of the Association who shall hold office until their successors are elected to office; and the World Council may appoint Honorary Commodores from time to time as they shall see fit.

(4) The Executive Secretary shall be appointed by the elected members of the World Council and shall hold office for such term and upon such conditions as the World Council shall decide. He shall be situated at the Head Office of the Association and shall be responsible for the management of all business of the Association, subject to and in accordance with the Constitution, By-Laws, and the direction of the World Council, including

(a) the coordination of all inter-regional activities,

(b) the organization of all activities relating to World Championships,

(c) liaison between the Association, the I.Y.R.U., and all other yachting authorities, and

(d) liaison between the membership and the Chief Measurer.

(5) The World Council shall appoint, for such term as it shall decide, a Chief Measurer for the Association who shall rule on all questions

and challenges relating to the Rules, and shall issue Interpretations thereof deemed necessary by him. All such Interpretations shall be binding until approved, rejected, or modified by decision of the World Council, duly published to the members of the Association.

Regions

7. (1) The World Council may, as and when it deems it convenient for the administration of the affairs of the Association within a substantial area where several Districts are or may be established, constitute such area as a Region.

(2) The World Council, upon establishing a Region, shall appoint a Regional Executive Committee comprising of a Regional Chairman, Vice Chairman, and Executive Secretary, to hold office until their successors are elected.

(3) The Regional Executive Committee shall have those powers, vested in the World Council by this Constitution (other than the power to amend the Rules or this Constitution) as are specifically delegated to the Regional Executive by the Regional By-Law, including the power to appoint additional officers for such term as it may from time to time determine.

(4) The Regional Executive officers, other than the Executive Secretary, shall be elected annually by vote of the Chairman (or other officer authorized by him if he is unable to attend) of each District at the annual Regional meeting to be held at the head office of the Region or such other place as the Regional Executive Committee shall determine, and shall hold office until their successors are elected, and nothing shall preclude one of the District Chairman as also acting as the Regional Chairman.

(5) The Regional Executive Secretary shall be appointed by the elected members of the Regional Executive Committee, and shall hold office for such term and upon such conditions as the Regional Executive Committee shall decide. He shall be responsible for the management of the business of the Region, subject to and in accordance with the Regional Executive By-Law and the direction of the Regional Executive Committee, including

(a) the coordination of inter-District activities and events,

(b) liaison with the Executive Secretary of the World Council,

(c) issuance of Fleet Charters,

(d) maintenance of all records of the Region, and

(e) maintenance of all membership records and information, unless such duties are delegated to the District Secretary.

(6) The World Council may subdivide a Region into one or more Regions, may amalgamate two or more Regions or may add Districts to or delete Districts from any Region from time to time as may be required for the effective administration of the Association.

(7) In the event that a Regional Chairman shall be unable to attend any meeting of the World Council, the Executive Secretary of the region or such any other member of the Regional Executive Committee nominated for that purpose may attend and represent the Chairman and vote at such meeting of the World Council.

(8) Nothing shall preclude the Executive Secretary of a Region also serving as Executive Secretary of the World Council.

(9) The Regional Executive Committee may make By-Laws, subject to the provisions of this Constitution and the Regional Executive By-Laws of the World Council, for any purpose necessary to carry out the functions and responsibilities of such Region, and copies of all such By-Laws as are from time to time passed by any Regional Executive shall be filed with the Executive Secretary of the World Council.

Districts

8. (1) The World Council, on the recommendation of a Regional Executive Committee where applicable, shall by By-Law establish Districts in distinctive areas deemed appropriate and relevant, having regard to all considerations, including geography, language, distance, and population, for the development of the Laser Class and the fulfillment of the objects of the Association.

(2) The World Council, upon establishing Districts, shall appoint District Associations comprised of a District Chairman, a Vice Chairman, a Secretary, and a Treasurer, to hold office until their successors are elected.

(3) The District Association shall consist of the foregoing officers, and may appoint such additional officers to hold office for such term as it may determine.

(4) Each District shall be administered in accordance with and subject to the provisions of a Constitution of the District, approved by the World Council, or if the District has no Constitution, the District Association By-Law of the World Council; and the officers of each District Association shall be elected annually by the members of the

Association within the District in accordance with the provisions of the District Constitution or, in the absence thereof, the District Association By-Law.

(5) The boundaries of Districts may be varied by the World Council on the application of any District concerned, and one or more Districts may be amalgamated or any District may be subdivided into one or more Districts with the approval of the District Associations concerned.

(6) A District Association with the approval of the Chief Measurer may appoint a District Measurer for a District to assist the Chief Measurer in the conduct of his responsibilities and the enforcement of the Rules; and nothing precludes a District Measurer from acting as Measurer for more than one District. A District Measurer shall have the authority to rule on all questions and challenges relating to the Rules and Interpretations of the Chief Measurer, but he may not issue Interpretations except with the prior approval of the Chief Measurer.

(7) A District Association may make By-Laws, subject to the provisions of this Constitution, the Regional Executive By-Laws, and the District Association By-Law or District Association Constitution, for any purpose necessary to carry out its functions and responsibilities in the management of such District.

(8) If any District is within the jurisdiction of a National authority, such District Association shall, in addition to any other requirements of this constitution, be subject to such rules, regulations and directions of such National authority.

Fleets
9. (1) A Fleet may be granted a charter upon application to the Regional Executive Committee (or the World Council where the locality is outside a Region) by 6 or more members of the Association who are individual owners of Lasers within any area or club deemed appropriate, having regard to the locality where regular racing activity is easily accessible to members of that Fleet.

(2) Notwithstanding paragraph (1), a special Fleet may be chartered in any locality for the purposes of accommodating specific members of the armed forces, and educational institution, a junior program or any other non-profit organization.

(3) A Fleet Captain, and such other officers if any as the Fleet may

deem necessary, shall be elected annually from among the members of the Fleet in such manner as is prescribed by the Fleet, unless otherwise provided by the By-Laws, and shall be responsible to the District Association for the organization of the Fleet and the due compliance by the members of the Fleet with the provisions of the Constitution and By-Laws of the Association.

MEMBERSHIP AND DUES:

10. See Rule 26 of the Laser Rules.

11. (1) Any person may become a member of the Association by making application to the Executive Secretary, or the appropriate Regional Executive Secretary or District Secretary, as the case may be, and payment of the prescribed Association dues, provided that he has not been disqualified from membership for cause by decision of the World Council or under suspension from membership.

(2) An application for membership implies that the applicant undertakes and agrees to be bound by the Constitution and By-Laws of the Association upon being accepted to membership.

(3) A member of the Association *ipso facto* belongs to the District in which he normally sails, even though such place may not be his permanent residence; but such member, for valid reason and with the approval of both District Chairmen, may select instead the District in which he has his permanent residence.

(4) A member of the Association may become a member only of the Fleet in his District where he normally sails for the purpose of qualification, where required, for sanctioned events; and any dispute shall be settled by decision of the District Association which decision shall be final.

(5) The World Council may grant honorary membership in the Association, for such period as it determines, to any person who, through special contribution to the Class or through special relationship to the Association, is considered meritorious.

(6) The World Council may grant an honorary life membership to any member who has achieved, in the opinion of the World Council, international stature as a result of his yachting achievements.

(7) An honorary and an honorary life member are entitled to full privileges of membership, but are not required to pay the annual dues of the Association.

(8) Membership in the Association shall not be open to any company, partnership, group or other association unless specifically authorized in any case or class of cases by the World Council; and the World Council may impose such terms, conditions or qualifications to any such membership as it shall deem appropriate.

12. (1) Association dues shall be in the amount determined by and shall be payable within the time prescribed by By-Law of each Region or District, as determined by the World Council, and shall include all amounts required for World Council, Region and District purposes as determined by each authority.

(2) The Association may ask for special contributions in addition to dues, provided any such contribution shall be for a specific purpose and shall not be mandatory.

(3) Dues shall be collected by the Regional Executive Secretary, but the World Council may authorize the District Secretary to collect such dues under such terms and conditions as to reporting and accounting as may be required.

SUSPENSION AND REMOVAL FROM OFFICE

13. A member may be suspended by the World Council, on the recommendation of a District Association, for gross violation of the Rules or By-Laws, for committing an unlawful act in relation to the Association or one of its members, or for any unsportsmanlike conduct contrary to the interests of the members of the Association. The duration of the suspension shall be fixed by the World Council but may not exceed two years, and a suspended member shall during such period be precluded from racing or enjoying any other rights of membership.

14. A Regional or District officer may be removed from office by the World Council for a willful and unjustifiable act of commission or omission detrimental to the Association or to its members.

APPEALS

15. Any dispute arising in relation to fleets, districts, regions, eligibility to race, the interpretating of this Constitution, the By-Laws or similar matter, other than any dispute as to the interpretation of the Rules or any protest within the jurisdiction of the applicable racing rules, may be made to the World Council whose decision shall be final and binding.

ADVISORY COUNCIL

16. The President and Vice President of the World Council and two persons nominated by Performance Sailcraft Inc. shall constitute the Advisory Council and shall assist and cooperate with the World Council in the carrying out of their responsibilities, and shall have the responsibilities as set forth in para. 18 hereof and para. 27 of the rules.

BY-LAWS

17. The World Council may make By-Laws for the purpose of carrying out the objects of this Constitution and of the Association and, without restricting the generality of the foregoing, may make By-Laws

(a) amending the Rules of the Laser Class, hereby established as By-Law 1 of the Association, as provided in paragraph 22 thereof;

(b) respecting the establishment of Regions, and the powers of the Regional Executive Committees;

(c) delegating specific powers of the World Council to Regional Executive Committees;

(d) respecting the establishment of Districts and the powers of District Associations;

(e) respecting the Constitutions and By-Laws of District Associations;

(f) respecting registration of members and collection of dues;

(g) respecting the measurement of boats and measurement fees;

(h) respecting the conduct of championship and other regattas, including the classification of regattas and the eligibility of members for major racing events;

(i) respecting the acceptance of deeds of gift of trophies;

(j) changing the Headquarters of the Association; and

(k) respecting the procedures for meetings of the World Council and Regional Executive Committees, including the conduct of business by mail or other means of communication.

AMENDMENTS

18. (1) This Constitution may be amended by the World Council, with the approval of the Advisory Council, provided that at least two-thirds of the District Associations have approved such proposed amendment at Special General Meetings of the District Associations called for that

purpose, or at the Annual Meetings of the District Associations, provided not less than ten days notice of such proposed amendment has in each case been given.

(2) Amendments to the Constitution shall be submitted for vote of each District

(a) by direction of the World Council; or

(b) by direction of the Executive Secretary where notice of motion signed by at least twenty members has been submitted to and approved by at least two District Associations.

TRANSITION PROVISIONS

19. (1) This Constitution shall come into force on the date of the approval thereof by the Association in accordance with the provisions of Article XVIII of the Laser Association Constitution enacted September 30, 1972; and thereupon the said Constitution enacted September 30, 1972, shall be repealed and the officers of the Association elected and appointed under the provisions of the Constitution enacted September 30, 1972, shall be deemed to be the first officers of the World Council under the within Constitution, to hold office until their successors are appointed or elected, as the case may be.

(2) On the coming into force of this Constitution each District and each Fleet established under the Constitution enacted September 30, 1972, shall be deemed to be Districts and Fleets within the meaning of this Constitution, and all officers and Fleet Captains of such Districts and Fleets shall be deemed to be the first officers and Fleet Captains of such Districts and Fleets under this Constitution until their successors are appointed or elected, as the case may be.

(3) All actions of the Executive Committee or other officers of the Association, including any District officer, made or performed pursuant to the said Constitution enacted September 30, 1972, shall be deemed to be validly done for the purpose of the within Constitution to the same extent as though same were carried out in accordance with the provisions hereof.

BY-LAW 1: RULES — AMENDED NOVEMBER 11, 1974

ONE-DESIGN PRINCIPLE

1. The design and development of the Laser was directed to the creation of a strict one-design class where the true test is between helmsmen and not boats, and therefore any alteration of the hull form, construction, equipment, spars, sail or running rigging, as supplied by the builder, except as is specifically authorized by these Rules is a breach of these Rules, not only in spirit but in substance, and is prohibited.

DEFINITION

2. In these Rules, "builder" means any manufacturer duly authorized or licensed to build the Laser by The International Yacht Racing Union (IYRU) with the approval of Performance Sailcraft International Company Limited (PSI).

HULL AND DECK

3. The hull and deck shall be built from tooling manufactured and supplied by PSI and shall be constructed in accordance with the specifications of PSI approved by the IYRU.

CENTREBOARD

4. The centreboard shall only be supplied by the builder and shall be of wood or other material approved by PSI and the IYRU.

5. A rope handle passing through not more than two holes of maximum diameter 12 mm (½"), above the deck when the centreboard is lowered, is permitted.

6. Subject to Rule 4, nothing herein shall preclude minor adjustments to the centreboard by way of sharpening the trailing edge, refinishing or repairing damage provided that the centreboard

    (a) can be readily moved up and down at all times,

    (b) has stops affixed which preclude its protrusion below the bottom of the boat more than 680 mm (26.8") measured along the trailing edge as shown on the measurement diagram, and

    (c) has maximum thickness, and profile, in accordance with the measurement diagram.

7. A line or shock cord may be tied or hooked through a small hole in the upper forward corner of the centreboard to the mast, an existing

fitting on the mast or the cunningham fairlead to prevent loss in the event of capsize, but no wedges or other fittings may be used in any other way than as supplied by the builder.

RUDDER
8. The rudder and rudder head shall only be supplied by the builder, and the rudder shall be of wood or other material approved by PSI and the IYRU.
9. The rudder blade shall have a downhaul.
10. Subject to Rule 8, nothing herein shall preclude minor adjustments to the rudder by way of sharpening the trailing edge, refinishing or repairing damage, provided that the rudder under-water profile, maximum thickness, and the included angle (of not more than 78) between the lower edge of the rudder head and the leading edge of the rudder blade, comply with the rudder measurement diagram.

TILLER
11. The tiller and tiller extension are not restricted in any way except that the tiller shall be capable of removal from the rudder head, and shall be straight.
12. The tiller shall have a cleat for the downhaul of any type or material.

FITTINGS
13. No fittings, wedges or other attachments may be affixed to the hull or deck, other than the fittings supplied by the builder, except the following:
    (a) The single *mainsheet block* supplied by the builder may be removed and replaced by either:
        (1) one *mainsheet swivel cam cleat* RWO model 195L, with cams of plastic or metal, and mounted as shown on the measurement diagram,
        or
        (2) a *single ratchet block,* of any type, mounted as shown on the measurement diagram; and mainsheet clam or cam cleats of any type may be mounted on the deck on each side of the cockpit;
    (b) *inspection ports* not exceeding 152 mm (6″) in diameter may be installed on the deck or in the cockpit to provide access to the hull cavity, provided that any inspection port is fitted with water-tight,

threaded covers (and bayonet mounted ports are deemed to be not threaded). A compass may not be attached to or mounted through an inspection port;

(c) *clips* of any kind or ties may be affixed for use only for securing paddles or an anchor in the cockpit or on the deck;

(d) *a self-bailing device* as supplied only by the builder may be added;

(e) the sheet metal screws in the traveller blocks may be replaced with bolts;

(f) the *traveller eyes* may be repositioned provided that no part of the eyes may be farther apart than 1067 mm (42″) measured on a line parallel to the aft edge of the deck nor closer together than 965 mm (38″). Also, no part of the eyes may be positioned closer than 235 mm (9¼″) to the after edge of the deck nor farther forward than 290 mm (11½″) from that edge; and

(g) *metallic clam cleats* (not cam cleats) may be substituted for the plastic clam cleats supplied by the builder for the traveller, outhaul and cunningham. The size and design must be the same as those supplied by the builder.

SHEETS AND LINES

14. Any sheets or lines may be substituted for those supplied by the builder, but no additional sheets or lines, unless specifically authorised, may be added. Sheets or lines in whole or in part of wire are prohibited. Each sheet or line must be one continuous length of line of uniform diameter. In addition:

(a) the *mainsheet* shall be attached to the becket on the block at the end of the boom and shall be reeved through all sheaves on the traveller and boom. While racing, the sheet shall not be controlled from aft of the forward block on the boom, except to facilitate a tack or gybe. Leading the sheet through the final block aft of the centreboard is optional;

(b) the *traveller* shall be one piece of line rigged in the form of a closed loop as supplied by the builder except that the line may be knotted instead of using a spliced loop. The end of the line forward of the clam cleat may be formed into a loop or knot for added purchase. No attachments, knots or other devices are permitted which would further assist or prevent free movement of the traveller block on the traveller;

(c) the *outhaul* shall be one piece of line which shall be rigged only as follows: It shall be dead-ended either at the fairlead on the end of the boom, or the clew of the mainsail (or a quick release snap-hook if used) passed between there two for as many purchases as the helmsman may require, and then lead forward to the cleat. After passing through the cleat, the free end may be taken to the mast but not to the deck;

(d) the *clew of the mainsail* may be tied to the boom in any manner provided no blocks or any fixed fittings are added;

(e) the *outhaul* and *clew tie-down* may be rigged to a snaphook for quick release in docking or in an emergency; and

(f) the *cunningham* line shall be one piece of line. It may be deadended at the gooseneck fitting, led through the cunningham grommet, then through the deck fairlead to the cleat. Additional purchase may be obtained by forming a loop in the line or using an existing fitting (such as the bridge of the clam cleat). However, no additional pieces of line, or additional fittings of any kind are permitted.

EQUIPMENT

15. No additional equipment may be affixed to any part of a Laser except the following:

(a) *storage bags* or receptacles may be attached to the inside of the cockpit;

(b) *one compass* may be mounted on the deck or in the cockpit, provided that the hull cavity is not pierced by other than the fasteners;

(c) *wind indicators* may be attached as follows:

(1) a wind indicator may be attached to the top of the mast provided that the water-tight integrity of the mast is maintained and the sail is not cut;

(2) in addition one wind indicator may be affixed anywhere to the boat, its boom, spars or equipment; and

(3) ribbons, wool or similar wind indicators may be attached to the sail; and

(d) the *hiking strap* as supplied by the builder may be padded and may be held taut by the use of a shock cord attached to the aft end of the strap and to the fittings at the aft end of the cockpit.

SAIL

16. No sail, including a replacement sail, is permitted unless it was purchased, when new, from the builder, or a duly authorised dealer.

17. No person may recut any sail or otherwise change or affect any aspect of the sail or pierce the sail for attaching anything to the mast for any reason other than effecting necessary repairs or placing racing numbers thereon.

18. One window may be installed in accordance with the measurement diagram.

Class Emblem and Sail Numbers

19. The class emblem shall be glued, sewn or silkscreened to each side of the sail, back to back, in the third panel from the head.

20. The registration number of each boat, as molded into the deck under the bow eye or into the transom, shall be the sail number of the boat. The sail number shall be glued, sewn or otherwise clearly marked to each side of the sail, placed parallel to the seam, with the number on the starboard side placed above that on the port side, in accordance with the IYRU Racing Rules.

The numbers shall be of the following minimum dimensions:

Height	300 mm (11¾")
Width	200 mm (8")
Thickness	45 mm (1¾")
Space between adjoining numbers	60 mm (2⅜")

The sails of all boats numbered after 2000 and all replacement sails shall have the numbers in the fourth panel from the head.

Mast and Boom

21. The mast, boom and all fittings attached thereto by the builder including the boom vang jamming block shall be supplied only by the builder and may not be drilled or altered or otherwise changed except that

(a) the angle of the boom vang jamming block may be changed by an additional shackle; and

(b) the boom vang jamming block may be reversed and keyed to the boom, but one block must be attached directly to the mast and the other to the boom.

22. No mast which has a permanent bend may be used at any time.

23. No attachments, fittings or devices may be used which affect or may affect the position or rake of the mast and nothing may be placed or wedged in the mast cavity other than the mast, but

(a) to prevent abrasion, a collar of uniform thickness not exceeding

0.5 mm and not wider than 25 mm placed around the entire circumference of either the mast or mast cavity is permitted,

(b) the mast or mast cavity may be lubricated, and

(c) tape or other bushing material may be applied to both the plastic end cap and/or the collar of the upper mast section to ensure a snug fit. The tape or bushing material may only be used on that portion of the plastic parts that actually slide into the lower section. Taping above the collar to fair the collar into the mast is prohibited.

REPAIRS AND REPLACEMENTS

24. (a) In the event of damage to hull, deck, centreboard, rudder, mast or boom, necessary repairs may be made thereto without violation of these Rules provided such repairs are made in such a way that the essential shape or other characteristics are not materially affected. In the event of the failure of any fitting, or the replacement of fittings as authorised by these Rules, the same or a replacement thereof shall be replaced in the same position as the fitting which failed, or as close to the same position as is structurally feasible.

(b) No treatment may be applied to the hull of a boat for the intended purpose of improving its performance, but nothing shall prohibit the repainting of a hull which requires refinishing.

SAILING REQUIREMENTS

25. (a) No part of the helmsman or crew may be placed forward of the mast while racing.

(b) Nothing shall prohibit two persons from racing a Laser, provided that both persons sail together for the entire regatta and do not alternate at the helm.

CLASS ASSOCIATION MEMBERSHIP

26. No person is permitted to race a Laser in any fleet, interfleet, District or other sanctioned event unless he is a current member of the International Laser Class Association (and a member of a District Laser Association duly established in accordance with the Constitution is *ipso facto* a member of the International Laser Class Association).

CLOTHING AND EQUIPMENT

27. (a) For the purposes of paragraph 3(b) of Rule 22 of the IYRU Racing Rules, the total weight of clothing and equipment worn or

carried by a helmsman shall not exceed 11 kilograms (24.2 lbs.) when wet, and the World Council may by by-law:

(1) define the method of weighing clothing or equipment,

(2) specify the nature of any clothing or equipment which may be used for the purposes of adding weight (herein called 'wadding'),

(3) restrict the weight of clothing which may be worn or carried for the purposes of protection from the elements,

(4) exempt wet suits from being weighed provided they meet safety requirements as specified, and

(5) restrict the use of wadding by competitors of any age or weight or in any other circumstances which in the interests of safety or the welfare of the Class it shall consider appropriate.

(b) In the event that a Laser shall carry a crew, such crew may not carry clothing or equipment (other than a life jacket) except for the purposes of protection from the elements, and any by-law passed pursuant to clause (3) of subparagraph (a) shall apply.

AMENDMENTS

28. Amendments to these Rules shall be approved by each of:

(a) the World Council,

(b) the Advisory Council,

(c) at least two thirds of the District Associations at special general meetings thereof called for that purpose, or at the annual meetings thereof, provided no less than ten days notice of such proposed Rule change has in each case been given, and

(d) the IYRU

Measurement Diagrams

All dimensions shown in millimeters

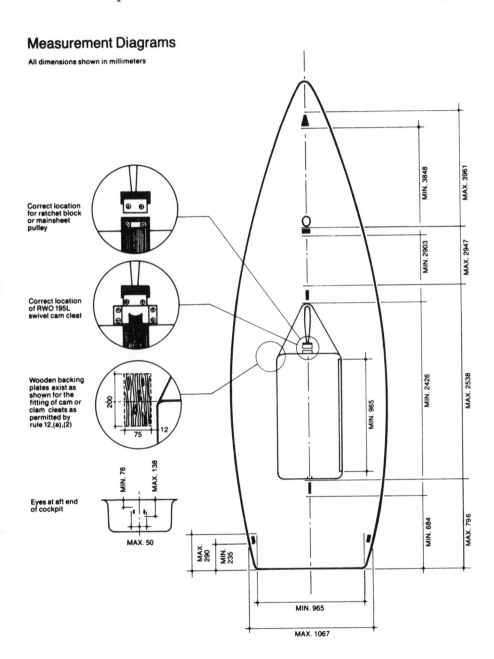

Correct location for ratchet block or mainsheet pulley

Correct location of RWO 195L swivel cam cleat

Wooden backing plates exist as shown for the fitting of cam or clam cleats as permitted by rule 12,(a),(2)

Eyes at aft end of cockpit

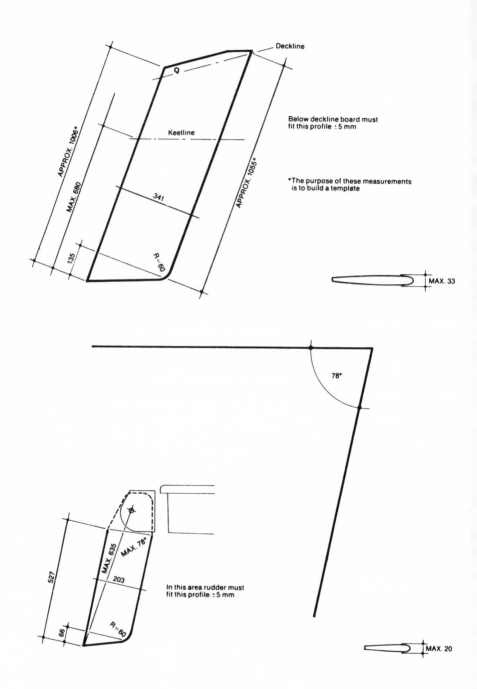

Deckline

Q

Keelline

Below deckline board must
fit this profile ±5 mm

*The purpose of these measurements
is to build a template

APPROX. 1006*

MAX. 680

APPROX. 1055*

341

135

R = 60

MAX. 33

78°

MAX. 635

MAX. 78°

527

203

66

R = 60

In this area rudder must
fit this profile ±5 mm

MAX. 20

All dimensions shown in millimeters

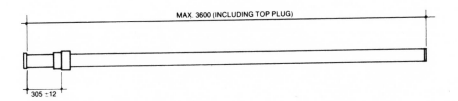

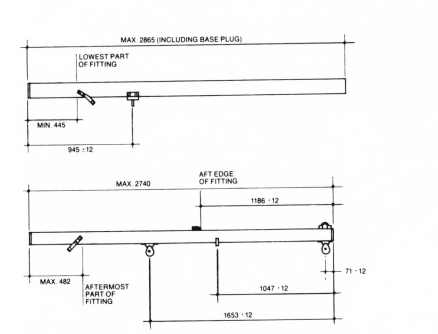

All dimensions shown in millimeters

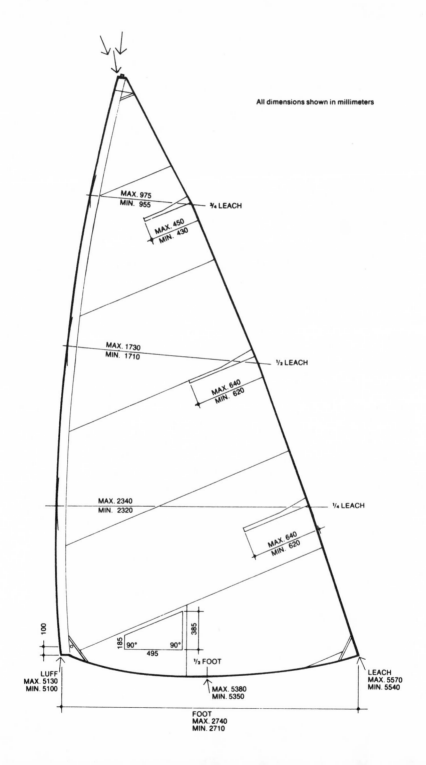

All dimensions shown in millimeters

MAX. 975
MIN. 955

¾ LEACH

MAX. 450
MIN. 430

MAX. 1730
MIN. 1710

½ LEACH

MAX. 640
MIN. 620

MAX. 2340
MIN. 2320

¼ LEACH

MAX. 640
MIN. 620

100

185   90°   90°   385
        495   ½ FOOT

LUFF
MAX. 5130
MIN. 5100

MAX. 5380
MIN. 5350

LEACH
MAX. 5570
MIN. 5540

FOOT
MAX. 2740
MIN. 2710

Appendix 5:
Laser Construction Particulars
The Laser Record

Laser Construction Particulars

The Laser is produced in two pieces with a fiberglass sandwich deck and a uniform single laminate hull, reinforced with stringers. The sandwich deck is made up of an initial glass laminate on a layer of ivory colored gelcoat. All the horizontal surfaces are then reinforced with Airex (foam core) and covered with a final laminate. The Airex, apart from providing exceptional rigidity, also gives the boat positive buoyancy with a specific gravity lighter than if built in wood.

The hull and deck are glued together with an additional 350 lb. of positive flotation included in the cavity between them. All fittings on the hull and deck have backing plates and all the self-tapping screws are stainless steel. The hull molds, deck molds, and glue jigs are all produced from master plugs in Pointe Claire, Canada and are shipped to Laser factories around the world.

The Laser's specifications are:

length overall	13′10½″	4.23 m.
waterline	12′6″	3.81 m.
beam	4′6″	1.37 m.
weight	130 lb.	58.97 kg.

The mast and boom are anodized aluminum. The mast consists of two pieces which, when joined, produce a tapered effect and a total length of 20′1″.

The sail is 76 square feet (actual), loose footed and has a sleeved luff which slides over the mast. The sail is three ounce Dacron and made to the design of Hans Fogh. As of September, 1974, all panels are cut to this design by a computer controlled cutting machine and the seams are ultrasonically welded in place to be sewn and hand worked by selected sail finishers at production points around the world.

The centerboard is a NASA 0009 airfoil shape and fits into the identically shaped centerboard trunk. The rudder is also a 0009 airfoil shape and lifts to avoid damage on beaching. The tiller is removable from the rudder head.

The Laser Record

Designed 1970.

First Prototype, November, 1970.

Winner, America's Tea Cup One-of-a-Kind, November, 1970.

First production boats, Montreal, March, 1971.

First North American Championship, October, 1971; 88 competitors.

Start-up California production, April, 1972.

Start-up UK production, June, 1972.

First UK Open, November, 1972; 65 competitors.

IYRU grants provisional International status, November, 1972.

US Nationals, August, 1973; 236 entries.

10,000th Laser produced, October, 1973.

Start-up New Zealand production, November, 1973.

Start-up Australia production, February, 1974.

IYRU grants full International status, July, 1974.

Start-up Ireland production, August, 1974.

20,000th Laser produced, September, 1974.

First World Championship, (Bermuda) October, 1974; 109 entries.

Start-up Brazil production, November, 1974.

Start-up Japan production, 1975.

A fleet of 109 representing 24 countries gathered in Bermuda in October, 1974, for the first World Championship.

Appendix 6:
The Laser World Championship

(1) **Peter Commette,** U.S., 4-5-1-12-5-73-1, 27.5 points.
(2) **Norm Freeman,** U.S., 7-22-6-2-29-13-12, 62 points.
(3) **Chris Boome,** U.S., 9-2-17-40-10-36-3, 77 points.
(4) **Hugo Schmidt,** U.S., 31-19-12-6-64-4-5- 77 points.
(5) **Carl Buchan,** U.S., 2-24-3-25-31-20-6, 80 points.
(6) **Gordy Bowers,** U.S., 12-1-2-30-36-39-4, 84.75 points.
(7) **Mark Duane,** U.S., 27-51-14-13-24-1-14, 92.75 points.
(8) **John Dane,** U.S., 22-15-11-11-39-28-16, 103 points.
(9) **Dick Tillman,** U.S., 11-9-DSQ-3-3-42-36, 104 points.
(10) **Jim Hahn,** U.S., 1-3-4-49-74-50-2, 108.75 points.
(11) **Gary Jobson,** U.S., 21-12-33-5-7-DSQ-40, 118 points.

Bermuda News Bureau

Peter Commette (19153) is shown after crossing the finish line in one of the early races of the seven-race series.

Peter Commette, 20, of Middletown, New Jersey, was the overall winner of the First Laser World Championship with an outstanding record of 4-5-1-12-5-73-1.

(12) **Ward McKimm,** Canada, 53-54-9-8-15-22-15, 122 points.

(13) **Jeff Boyd,** Canada, 34-38-DSQ-24-2-5-20, 123 points.

(14) **Rick Kern,** U.S., DSQ-17-22-15-46-18-9, 127 points.

(15) **Charles Horter,** U.S., 8-13-29-46-38-33-11, 132 points.

(16) **Laurent Quellet,** Switzerland, 44-7-DNF-26-61-7-7, 152 points.

(17) **Alex Kimball,** U.S., 46-42-43-17-16-8-30, 156 points.

(18) **Jamie Kidd,** Canada, 13-30-40-41-12-53-23, 159 points.

(19) **Scooter Kinsey,** U.S., DSQ-47-23-31-25-16-21, 163 points.

(20) **Stephen West,** Bermuda, 14-23-27-92-26-34-43, 167 points.

Bermuda News Bureau photographs by Eric Johnson and Roland Skinner

Close and intense racing marked the World Championship, which was sponsored by the International Laser Association, the Royal Bermuda Yacht Club and Performance Sailcraft International.

Top prize for the First Laser World Championship, which was held in Bermuda from October 13-19, 1974, was the handsome Bermuda Trophy, designed by Jacques Giard. It stands 17 inches high and is comprised of eight one-inch-thick clear acrylic modules, the upper halves of which symbolize a fleet of Lasers.